THE
Mathis
Maxims

. . . .

Lessons in Leadership

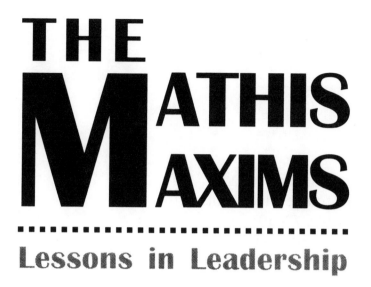

THE Mathis Maxims

Lessons in Leadership

by Larry L. Mathis

Leadership Press
1020 Holcombe Blvd., Suite 1107
Houston, TX 77030
713-795-5800

Leadership Press
1020 Holcombe Blvd., Suite 1107
Houston, TX 77030
Phone: 713-795-5800
Fax: 713-795-4417

ISBN: 1-890549-16-9

Dedication

This book is dedicated to Diane. Without her insistence, persistence, and assistance, it would not have been written. It would not have been published.

Author's Note

Maxims are necessarily generalizations. I know all the problems with generalizations. No generalization is totally accurate; there are exceptions to every generalization. While "physician executive" is an oxymoron in *The Mathis Maxims,* I know that there are doctors in our health system who are performing superbly in executive roles. I know that the reader will be able to cite other exceptions to some of the maxims, perhaps exceptions to all of them. However, with all the problems of generalization, I believe my maxims are true for organizations—generally true.

This work is not about precision of dates and times; it is a product of my memory. As such, it is subject to error. Others who participated in these events may recall them differently. I would not argue with their interpretation, but simply say that I wrote about them as I remembered and interpreted them. In error or not, this is the way I remember it all.

TABLE OF CONTENTS

CEO

Introduction

When I was thirty-nine years old, I was selected by the CEO search committee to become the fifth chief executive officer in the history of the internationally renowned The Methodist Hospital in Houston. All my professional dreams came true. After a grueling, twelve-year slog up the organization, my "fast track" had led to the corner office. Along the way, I had learned some hard lessons about leadership, about organizations, and about, as Texas' outrageously funny sports writer Dan Jenkins says, "life its ownself." At that happy moment, I realized I was about to learn a lot more.

I started a journal. I wanted to record, just for myself, those things that I had learned to be true. Over the next fourteen years of my tenure as a CEO, I wrote the truth as I saw it. Those truths were usually written in the form of maxims. They ranged over the peaks and valleys of the organizational landscape, touching on physician executives (an oxymoron), executive recruitment (you don't get better people, just different people), and boss/subordinate conflicts (the subordinate is always wrong), among many others. They touched upon life, wisdom, love, and folly. After several years, I had a serious collection of Mathis maxims (though not all maxims were serious). I shared some of the maxims with friends and colleagues, who encouraged me to share them with others. I decided to put them together in a speech for young, aspiring managers and executives. Several groups of young people received the talk very well, but I realized that younger managers just don't have the organizational or life experience to fully understand things like executive-suite warfare. I started giving the talk to more seasoned executives. With them, the maxims hit home. They had been there, seen that, done that, felt that. They encouraged me to publish them.

Each of the maxims stands alone. None requires additional comment. But, each of them is the product of excruciating experience. It is those experiences that father the truths. And in those experiences are lessons that I hope can be of value to those who read them. After each maxim, I write about the circumstance of its genesis. In those stories are warning markers for up-and-coming young executives who just might avoid the mistakes I made to learn a truth. In those stories are also, I hope, some comfort for those who have been through the wars.

The Man
In
The Maxims

The Man in the Maxims

It is raining today in Houston—one of those gray and sultry rains that seem to go listlessly on forever. I watch it through the window in my home office as I write at my computer. I'm wearing sweat pants and an oversized T-shirt that says, "Life is Good" on its front. I can't help but grin. I am fifty-six years old, reasonably healthy, happily married, and financially independent. I have successfully completed an executive odyssey that ended honorably and well, leaving me in the position of autonomy I planned for and promised myself I would achieve by age fifty-five. And, I have just finished writing the story of the final maxim. But, while the maxims are written, the book is not complete. I did not spring onto the stage as a fully formed and opinionated CEO. There is a man in these maxims.

The grin is a little too smug, given what I know life can do to the smug, but some of it comes from thinking back to the beginning. As my computer keyboard clicks away, I remember the dictating equipment in my office as administrative resident at Methodist—it was a plastic belt, which was etched by a stylus as I dictated. I was there even before the IBM Selectric typewriter arrived. "Wite-Out" and carbon paper were in full use. That really dates me, but I see it now so clearly.

The soft plastic click of the keys matches the steady fall of the rain. Graduate school. The army years. College. High school and boyhood. Back I go over the times and events that formed me, the episodes that shaped me and led to that strange epiphany in front of the hospital's mosaic mural and the launching of my career.

The sky was perfectly clear as I peaked out the window from my tiny room on May 29, 1948. It was going to be a great day! It was my fifth birthday (a date I was later to learn that I shared with Bob Hope and John F. Kennedy).

We lived in Pittsburg, Kansas, in a part of the state that had more in common with the hills and hollows of the Ozarks than it did with the great wheat plains for which the state is known. Pittsburg was a delightful town of about 18,000 people. Its main claim to fame is its college, then Kansas State Teacher's College, now pretentiously Pittsburg State University. Pittsburg was built on the second small town model—a single, central main street—rather than a town square. Such streets are usually named Main, but ours was Broadway. The best side of Broadway to live on was the West side. We lived on the East side, a block from the railroad tracks. Our small house was really a one bedroom something—shack is too unkind, cottage way overstates it. My mom had arranged a party for our back yard and all my friends were coming at noon. I couldn't wait.

Five years old is an important age. It is on the verge of really big things—like kindergarten. On that beautiful day, I had no cares, nothing on my mind other than the fun of my birthday party on a Spring day.

The kids began to arrive, carrying cards and packages. All of them were uncommonly clean and slicked down, a fact that fairly shouted out as contrary to the customary. There must have been twenty kids at the party, with assorted mothers to pour the Kool-Aid, scoop the ice cream, and cut the cake, while a few younger siblings crawled around the fringes. First, we had ice cream and cake. It didn't take my cousin, Karen, ten minutes to get sick and throw up. But we didn't mind, everyone knew she was pretty, but delicate. Opening the cards and presents was next. I don't remember any of the gifts I received except for one, but I do remember the wonderful feeling of being the center of attention while kids you like give you good stuff.

The gift I remember was given to me by Teddy, who lived up the street. It was a croquet set. Everyone could play! We, mother assisted, set up the wickets and posts in the back yard under the elms. It was a great game—I was winning. Teddy's turn came and he smacked the mallet against his red wooden ball with all the might a five-year old could bring to bear. What he thought he was doing, I have no idea. The ball cut a red streak through the grass, hit the bricked street and landed between parked Dodges on the far side. "I'll get it." I yelled. Laughing, and with a real sense of exhilaration I can still remember, I dashed across the street, grabbed the ball and ran back into the street—right into the path of old Mr. Huff's Ford. Bam. Darkness.

Dad was standing over me. When I awoke on his and Mom's bed, my Mother's hand was on my brow. My head ached unbearable and I didn't want to move any part of my body because I was afraid of what it would feel like. A man I didn't know was there. He told Dad that nothing was broken and he thought that a little rest would be all I'd need to get back to normal. As it turned out, that old Kansas doctor's diagnosis by examination, without benefit of lab work, x-rays, CT scans was absolutely correct.

The lasting impression of being hit by a car during my fifth birthday party was not to be on my body. It was my psyche that absorbed the lesson: Life can go from exhilaration to catastrophe (or as I thought then, "from good to bad") in no time at all. It was the first of many near misses to come. Those events would teach me about the uncertainties of life and its ability to deal unequally and unjustly with us all.

5

My Mathis grandparents came to the United States from Switzerland. My father and his brothers always swore that we were descended from royalty there. They had the Mathis coat of arms, a knight's helmet and shield imposed upon a royal blue and gold lily, to prove it. When the German text on the reverse of the coat of arms was translated later, it cited Florian, Geovanni, and Christian Mathis who in the 1500s were commissioners in various castles. I assume now, as I did back then, that those positions were far from royal; in fact, they were administrative. Which, if true, means I come honestly and genetically by my profession.

My grandfather, another and later Christian Mathis, grew up in Jenaz, a village in the high Alps. His wife-to-be lived just up the rail line in Klosters. Christian Mathis married Ursula Nett in the alt kirche (old church) in DaVos on August 16, 1903. My grandmother always told her grandkids that it was so cold that a man froze to death on her wedding day—in August! DaVos is another stop on the Alpine railroad beyond Klosters. Today, those towns are known as chic-chic international, jet-set, ski resorts; back then they were known for high sparse meadows, rock and ice. They had three children by the time my grandfather decided to take the family to the United States. Family lore has it that he believed that gold lay in the streets of America. Unfortunately, he found none. What he found was hard work on the railroad and later manual labor on a farm in eastern Nebraska. He died of stomach cancer before I was born. He never learned to speak English. His legacy was a wife left in poverty and eleven children for the New World.

My father's name was "Henry William George Washington deleted Mathis." That is what it actually says on his birth certificate. There is a line drawn through Washington and the word "deleted" is written above it. He was born on George Washington's birth date, 22 February 1913.

6

Apparently, his immigrant parents wanted to honor the father of their new country by naming the little boy for him, but thought better of it. He was the fourth son and was somewhere in the middle of the pack of eleven. He left home when he was twelve years old because, he said, he couldn't get enough to eat with all those other kids around. He was working as a stock boy in a grocery store in Tecumseh, Nebraska, in a job he often said he would have done for the rest of his life if they would agree to pay him $100 a month (they wouldn't), when he saw an unusually attractive brunette walk by.

The VanLaninghams were of Dutch decent, but the family tree is also sprinkled with numerous German names. When they reached America is unclear; but the family left Illinois in a covered wagon in 1868 and settled in Johnson County, Nebraska. My "grandpa Van" was Marion Oliver VanLaningham, the first child in the family born in Nebraska. He married Cora Auker December 11, 1890. They lived and farmed the rich soil around Tecumseh, had eight children—the last of whom was Berneta Lucille, who some years later got noticed in front of a grocery store in town by a black-haired, black-eyed first-generation American. She became my mother.

My mother was nicknamed Benny. She was born in 1916. As the youngest child, she was doted upon and played with for the first years of her life. Unfortunately, her mother died of cancer when she was only six years old. Her older sister, Gladys, had just gotten married at the time and volunteered to take her little sister into her home. She grew up in Gladys' home in Nebraska and moved with Gladys and her husband to Chicago when she entered her teens. She attended and graduated from Chicago's Arlington Heights High School, where she developed a sense of presence and style that set her apart from the other girls in rural Nebraska. That style and presence was immediately attractive to the man who would become my father.

George Mathis and Berneta VanLaningham were married on 24 September 1936 in Tecumseh. Things were tough for them in those days. My father liked to say that things were just beginning to look up for him—car, new job in Lincoln, newly rented house—as the war revived the depressed economy, when his draft board sent greetings. Before he shipped out, I was on the way. He spent the rest of the war in the scenic South Pacific in such idyllic spots as Guadalcanal, Sipan, and Iwo Jima.

"BOY 10:31 AM SATURDAY SIX POUNDS 10 OUNCES BOTH FINE—PAT."

The telegram from Mom's friend reached Corporal Mathis on the day of my birth May 29, 1943. It would be more than two years before my father and I would have a chance to get acquainted.

Elk Creek, Nebraska, pronounced El Crick by those who lived there, is a very small town. At the end of World War II my Dad came home, reclaimed his wife and son in Lincoln, and moved us there. The town is a scattering of houses along a dry creek bed at one end and a railroad track at the other. A dirt main street divided a general store on one side from a liquor store, barber shop, and the Blue Moon Café on the other. What my father was thinking when he opened the "Blue Moon" I have no idea. "Was he thinking?" may be the more appropriate question. I remember it as a big building. Mom was always behind the counter, preparing food before the diner opened and serving the men in overalls after it did. Booths ranged along the right wall. Passing through the diner, you entered the "ballroom." It was dark in there and intimidating to a little kid. The floor was always gritty with compound Dad scattered around to make dancing easier, and at the very rear of the room, high up on the wall, the lighted, cellophane, crescent Blue Moon glowed. We lived under the diner; a pool hall was under the ballroom. Most nights I drifted off to sleep in our little room listening to the sound of cue balls connecting.

On Saturdays, the farmers came into town; that's when the diner was busiest, when the dancing under the blue moon got serious, and money changed hands in the pool hall. Early on one of those days, Mom took me across the street to the general store. It was one of those old fashioned stores—with barrels, piles of overalls, glass candy jars, creaky old wooden floors, and a cast iron stove. On a back aisle, there was a long series of glass containers with round tin lids. As Mom talked to the owner on the other side of the aisle, I opened the lid on the container with the sugar cookies in it and grabbed one. As I took my first bite, the old owner appeared at the end of the aisle—I was nailed red-handed. I did the only thing I could think of at the time: I ran.

I hid under my bed and listened with dread as Mom explained to Dad what had happened. He dragged me out into the light and told me we were going back to the store where I was going to apologize for the theft and work for the owner until I had worked off the value of that cookie. With a sick feeling in the pit of my stomach, I walked with my Dad back across that street, into the store, and up to the owner. Through streaming tears, I blubbered "I'm sorry I took your cookie" and volunteered to work it off. He looked at me sternly, then at my Dad. He said, "Well, I think you've learned a lesson." He gave me another sugar cookie.

We didn't stay long in Pittsburg the first time. We were there to celebrate my fifth, and nearly last, birthday, for me to complete kindergarten and part of first grade, and for my life to change radically. They took my Mom to Mount Carmel Hospital in a rush in January, 1949. I was really concerned. I wasn't told much except that Mom would be fine. Days later, I was relieved to see Dad's car pull into the drive-way and Mom get out—with a blanket-wrapped bundle in her arms. My sister, JoEllen, had arrived.

At five years and eight months of age, everything changed for me. I had been the sole center of attention in the Mathis family so long. My Mother stayed at home in those days and let me know in no uncertain terms that I was wonderful. As a result, I was a Mama's boy of the first order, one who didn't want to dance unless Mommy was watching. Now, sometimes I danced and Mom wasn't watching.

My early years brought me the wonders of many small towns as we followed my dad's peripatetic career from Elk Creek, Nebraska to Pittsburg, Kansas to Miami, Oklahoma, to Red Oak, Iowa, to Wray, Colorado, and back to Pittsburg.

It was in Miami, Oklahoma, (pronounced Miama for some reason) that I finished (barely) the first grade and began the second. The move from Kansas to Oklahoma was educationally traumatic for me. You see, Kansas educators believed the best way to teach a child to read was by sight; Oklahoma teachers believed in phonics. I had done well in reading at Washington Elementary School in Pittsburg, but was totally at a loss in Miami when my enormous, Germanic second grade teacher, Mrs. T, growled at me to "sound it out, sound it out" when I stumbled in reading. Oklahoma educators also believed in the caste system, based upon the ability to read: The best readers sat all day at the Red Bird table; the next best group of readers sat at the Blue Bird table; and, I perceived and Mrs. T seemed to agree, the scum of the earth sat at the Yellow Bird table. I was told to join the Yellow Birds. About thirty kids, roughly divided into thirds, were venerated or excoriated on their ability to "sound it out, sound it out," regardless of their accomplishments in math, science, sports, or their essential worth as individuals. Of one thing I was certain, I might be having trouble with a system of reading that was new to me, but I WAS NOT A YELLOW BIRD!

In Miami, we lived in a very nice one-story, two

bedroom white house that would probably have been called a bungalow when it was new in the 1920s. It was on our porch swing there that I found my Mom sitting every day as I came walking home from school. It was our time together to deal with my reading problem. Every day, right after school, sitting on that swing together, I would read to my Mom and "sound out" words I didn't know.

Soon, my reading began to improve. As a result of that improvement, I was treated to another of life's lessons. Mrs. T took note of my increasing ability to "sound out" words and, after a few weeks, promoted me to the Blue Bird table. You cannot imagine the sense of triumph, pride, and exhilaration I felt. Maybe I wasn't a Red Bird yet (which in my heart, I knew I was), but I was on my way. With all those feelings, plus relief at leaving the Yellow Birds behind, I took my place in a higher social order. I hadn't been at the Blue Bird table twenty seconds when my friend, Ben, another Blue Bird, looked at me with a mischievous glint in his eyes and then made a loud, vulgar noise with his tongue and lips. Mrs. T, whose back had been turned, spun on her over-sized heels, scanned the Blue Bird table, sized up the situation, reached out and grabbed me (ME) by the back of the shirt. She propelled me into the cloak room, took ping pong paddle in hand and whaled me as I cried and screamed "I didn't do it." She then dragged me back into the classroom and slammed me back down in my seat. At the Yellow Bird table!

Injustice. Punished for something I didn't do. My truthful denials ignored. Once scum, always scum, in Mrs. T's eyes. I wept. There are no tears like tears shed over injustice.

Wray is in eastern Colorado, which is more like flat western Kansas than everyone's mental image of that Rocky Mountain state. During my fourth grade year in that dusty little town, I learned about work, about the value of a dollar, and about feminine beauty. My Dad decided that at ten years of age I needed to learn about work. He thought it would be very instructive to me if I spent my Saturdays in janitorial service at his place of employment—a Case Farm Implements Quonset hut. My duties were to empty all trash bins, sweep and dust the front office, spread compound and sweep all the back-of-the-hut maintenance areas, and clean the bathroom, its sink and its toilet —the very worst part. When the job was done Dad then inspected my work. Invariably he pointed out an area that I had missed or done poorly. I would then, under supervision, redo my work. Finally, I was taken to the office, the cash register was solemnly opened, and I was given my day's wages. One dollar. Usually, I then went to the "five and dime" and bought my Mom a present and went to the ice cream parlor for a chocolate soda. I spent the Saturdays of my fourth grade year learning to dislike, but respect, hard and sometimes disgusting physical work and learning to appreciate what it can take to earn a dollar.

Our little house in Wray sat up on a slight rise. From it you could see across the street and down into a low pasture. A picturesque stream ran through it. Behind the house, there was a small out-building in which I built my secret club house and next to it was a large, horizontal white butane tank. Sometimes it was my Sherman tank from which I slew the Godless Hun; sometimes it was my pirate ship; sometimes I saddled it and, through sheer athletic ability, won my World Championship belt buckle in bull riding. And, at one enchanted gilded Western sunset, I sat there and watched a beautiful, blond, long-haired, long-legged girl ride down our street on a Palomino horse while her collie dog trotted along beside her. I had never seen anything so beautiful, so moving, or so golden in my life.

Finally, after a decade of moving to a different state every year we came back to Pittsburg to stay. It was the best place, in Mom and Dad's judgment, of all the places we had lived. It was small enough to be a good place for my sister and me to grow up; it was large enough, with 18,000 residents and the local college's 6,000 additional young people, to be interesting. We moved into another small, white, two-bedroom house, indistinguishable from all the others in the small towns where we had lived. I reentered Washington Elementary School, where I had last distinguished myself in kindergarten, as a fifth grader.

The Pittsburg years stretched from fifth grade to my graduation from college. Those years from 1953 to 1965—my formative ones—were spent in an innocent, protected, and isolated middle-American backwater. Doors were never locked—not houses, not cars. It was there (living across the street from a church may have had something to do with) that my Dad got religion. And when Dad got something, we all got it. Our family, in the great Baptist tradition, spent all of our non-working/non-school time at Church, whether we wanted to or not. In Pittsburg, racial tensions arose when some kid called another "Wop" or "Dago," not from interaction with the few black kids in our classes. Illegal drugs may have visited Pittsburg in those days, but they didn't find their way among any of my friends. Sex was something all the guys in my crowd hoped the older guys, or at least somebody, was getting. Those years were at the close of the Korean War and mostly before President Kennedy was assassinated. They were before Watergate took away our innocence and Vietnam took away our friends.

As I walked onto the playground at Washington Elementary, my twin pals from my prior years in Pittsburg, Larry and Gary, came rushing over. One took my books while the other starting yelling to the kids on the playground, "he's back." Feeling a little sheepish, but not indisposed to the idea of a triumphal return, I crossed the ball field with my friends, entered the building and began what would become a two-year relationship with a great teacher, Mrs. Tedlock.

I don't know why she was assigned to teach fifth grade that year and then taught sixth grade the following year. I don't think she liked us so much she couldn't bear to have us go on without her; I don't think it was a promotion. But, whatever the cause, I know that I benefited from having her spend those two important years really getting to know me. I don't remember how I was chosen, but I wound up editing our class paper and starring in our class drama for the local radio station. I suspect she had something to do with it. She told my parents that I had speech and drama talents which should be encouraged and a sense of humor that was going to get me in trouble. Years later when Pittsburg State University named me a distinguished alumnus, she told one of her friends "I didn't know what he would be, but I knew he would be something."

I would guess the Mathis family entered the middle class when we moved into the house at 108 West Forest. First of all, it was on the good side of Broadway—the west side. Sure, it was only one block west of Broadway, but it was the west side nonetheless. Second, the house had three, I said three, bedrooms! Let's savor that for a minute. That, basically, would be one bedroom for Mom and Dad, one bedroom for JoEllen, and one bedroom for ME. And, the house had two bathrooms! Finally, we didn't rent it, Dad bought it.

The neighborhood around our house was teeming with kids. Within a three-block radius, I counted 30 boys who were within one or two years of my age. Most of them were younger, the product of the baby boom, but there were also plenty who were already in Lakeside Junior High School. There must have been some girls too, but we mostly didn't notice them. On warm summer nights, you could always count on at least fifteen guys for a game of kick-the-can, punch-the-pig, or bicycle ditch'em. We played softball, baseball, and football, in their own seasons and with full teams, in the vacant lot behind the Shell station on Broadway. We flew our kites there, too. One year we all built racers for a soap box derby—Kansas style. We lined them up in the flat street at the side of my house and pushed them. The soap boxes with the biggest kids pushing won the races. When the sprints were over, we dragged our racers to the Shell lot for the finale: the destruction derby. Dickey, whose racer didn't win any sprints because it was made out of heavy army ammunition boxes, won the demolition event hands down. My racer was a graceful and delicate thing, made by stretching cotton sheets over a wooden frame then shellacking and painting it. It was bright red and, following the last event, torn to shreds.

We hiked and camped—first as Boy Scouts and later as Explorers. We attended scout and church camps. Our Baptist church camps did not permit co-ed camping in those days. The girls' camp was the first week; the boys' the second, with a full day between to insure that there was no possible fraternization. But, orientation for campers was held in the church sanctuary for all campers and their parents. I was titillated by the instructions for the girls: no two-piece bathing suits, bath robes to be worn to and from the pool, no shorts, no halters. My Methodist friends told me that their camp, which definitely was co-ed, was THE place to meet girls from all over the state. The contrast between the Baptist's rules and the Methodist Youth Fellowship experience sowed the seeds of my later conversion to Methodism.

We Baptists went to Grove, Oklahoma, to a camp on the Grand Lake of the Cherokees. On one bright sun shining morning on the parade ground, with campers in rows facing the flag, as we recited the pledge of allegiance, for me, the sunlight slipped into darkness. I put my hands on the shoulders of the kid in front of me, sank to my knees, and passed out. I was taken to the camp clinic. My temperature was 105 degrees.

They took me to a doctor in town, then they took me home to Pittsburg, where our family GP diagnosed the Asian Flu. I nearly died. I was weak and frail that entire summer as I, and as it turned out, a host of others around the world suffered through one of the worst flu epidemics in history. Close call. Healthy and active at camp one minute, gravely ill the next. The only bright spot that summer was that I learned to love books. I learned to read for pleasure. If I had been my normal, hyperactive, physical self, I would have never taken Mom's advice to get a library card. But during those long, long days of illness, reading was all I could do. My first two books were action stories, one the story of a hot-rodding teenager, the other a kids' biography of Crazy Horse. Book after book, I created my love affair with reading.

It was during a long Pittsburg summer that I first expressed entrepreneurial creativity. Sensing pent-up demand, I opened a casino in the shed next to our carport in the back yard. It really wasn't a casino, it was more of a carnival mid-way booth operation. I painted squares on the concrete floor with numbers (1s, 3s, 5s, and one 25) in each. The squares were small, the lines around them, thick. I set up a few pieces of wood to keep the contestants from getting too close to the squares and opened for business. It was a coin pitching game. Any coin would do. If a coin landed in a square, the pay-out was the multiple of the number in the square. If it landed on a line, the house kept the coin. First, I cleaned out the Larsen brothers, Tommy, Johnny, and Jimmy. All of their allowance for the week. Then I trimmed Chris and Mikey. Then Dennis from down the street. Then Charley. It was a sweet little operation and, if the Larsen brothers hadn't told my Dad how they lost their allowance, I might have developed a different attitude about gambling. The knock came at the shed door.

"Hi, Dad. What's up?'

"Nothing much. What's up in here?'

"Oh, just a little game I organized."

"Really, how do you play?"

In retrospect, I probably should have closed up shop right then; but I was flush with victory and cash (often a time of poor judgment). I told him how to play. He asked if he could have a shot at it. I said, "why sure." It took him twelve minutes to pocket the Larsens' allowance and every other cent I had. He then pitched a fifty cent piece and it landed dead in the center of the square marked 25. Payout—$12.50! The "house" didn't have any money, much less $12.50. My carnival- gaming days were over. The money went back to the Larsens, et al. I learned early what is was like to go from flush to flushed. I later watched it happen repeatedly in Houston in the 1980s.

In sum, mine was an idyllic boyhood on Forest Street, middle America.

My sports career with the Lakeside Junior High School Wild Cats was less than distinguished. I played eighth and ninth grade basketball and high jumped and pole vaulted on the track team. In basketball, my main concern was to avoid sitting at the very end of the bench. The cheerleaders had this special cheer that named all the players: "Reese, Reese, he's our man, if he can't do it, Bicknel can" and so on down the bench to the last man. I hated to hear, "Mathis, Mathis, he's our man, if he can't do it, nobody can." I usually moved up a place or two to avoid it. Bench work, like that, often required special forethought and action. In track, I actually won the pole vault in the dual meet with cross-town rival, Roosevelt. And, I placed in several meets in both the pole vault and the high jump, but I really wasn't any good at either. Football, to the great disappointment of my Dad, was out because I wasn't heavy enough.

Undistinguished in athletics, I was mediocre in

academics. The only two courses I remember vividly are algebra and home economics. I was one of thirty kids chosen for an early algebra class. We were chosen because we had been good at math in elementary school. I remember algebra vividly because it ruined me forever for higher math. At the end of my ninth grade year, I received a "C-" with several prior grading periods listing "Ds" on my report card. I left that course confused and terrified of algebra and anything more advanced. I got out of high school by taking only Geometry ("D"), and college with a modern math course ("C") which I put off taking until my junior year.

Home economics, you may think, is an unusual course for a junior high school boy. All of us eighth grade guys certainly agreed that it was highly unusual, not to mention unwanted and unmanly. But the Kansas Board of Education had more wisdom than we did; they ordained that in the eighth grade boys would be required to take home economics and girls would be required to take shop. For one semester we boys learned to set tables, to cook and to bake. We did huck toweling. We learned how to select vegetables and we had to memorize the parts of a side of beef. We learned to use a sewing machine. The things I learned in that all-boys home economics class were things that were useful and things that have stayed with me throughout my life. And, it is not a bad thing to teach girls to use a hammer, screw driver and wrench. When my daughters went off to college, I gave each of them a brand new tool box full of the implements and supplies necessary to fix common things in a dorm room. But, as enlightened as the home-ec.-for-boys/shop-for-girls policy was, it was still the 1950s. Our sewing machine project? Each boy was required to make his own shop apron.

During summers and part-time when school was in session, I worked at the 1106 Drive In. It was a local version of a Dairy Queen, with soft ice cream cones, malts, banana splits, root beer floats, and foot long hot dogs, the best sellers. The place was owned by an elderly Swedish-American couple from Wisconsin. The husband was a wonderful guy; the wife was a shrew. I handled the Drive In alone until it closed at night, when the shrew came in to check the cash register and inspect the place. She had developed a list of so many tasks that I found it impossible to get everything done, so every morning when I opened the 1106 for business, there was a prim little "you failed to" note waiting for me. It was only when I quit to start work at Runyon's Office Supply that my employers told me how much they thought of me and that I was the only one they trusted to handle the 1106 when they went out of town. It stayed with me a long time. While you're walking out the door is a strange time to learn that you are appreciated. Years later, when I was an executive, none of my employees ever got a "you failed to" note from me.

Teen Town was the name of the gathering spot for slow dancing and the dirty bop. I didn't have the rhythm or the self-confidence to do the dirty bop, but I box-waltzed every chance a got. I sure liked holding those soft and curvy girls while Johnny Mathis sang about the twelfth of never. By the eighth grade I was on the periphery of the popular clique. At one of the Thursday night dances, one of the "in" girls, who almost never spoke to me, came over to announce that Terry, a majorette, was interested in going steady with me. Whoa! I asked Terry to dance and then gave her my silver-plated I.D. bracelet. That's what made going steady official. I mooned over her all week. I was in love. I could not wait to get back to Teen Town the following Thursday to hold her on the dance floor again. When I arrived the following week, I was met by Terry's girl friend, the one who had conveyed the original message. With only a trace of pity, she informed me that Terry was now going steady with Bob and handed me my I.D. bracelet. Stunned, I croaked, "What happened?" She said

"You didn't call her, you didn't come to her classes and carry her books, you never came to her house." What? I thought once I plighted my I.D. bracelet, it was forever. Apparently, the bracelet was only the beginning, rather than an end in itself. That was my first inclination that there were some important unwritten rules about relationships with the opposite sex. And that the expectations at the beginning of any relationship should be understood before the I.D. bracelet changes hands.

I almost did not make it to high school. I pulled up to the stop sign on Broadway on my Whizzer, looked to the right down the street past the Food Town store, looked left toward the center of town. Nothing coming. I revved the engine to sprint across to the east side and smashed full tilt into a station wagon. The bike was crushed under the car's wheels and I went flying onto its hood, hit the windshield, broke off the side-view mirror with my shoulder, and landed on the far side in the street. The woman whose car I had plowed into had stopped, helped get me home, and insisted I go to the hospital for a checkup. I refused. I was okay. But, it was another close call.

My father's one ambition for me in life was that I play high school football. He had loved playing football and saw in me a way to relive his former glory years. He always told me that my high school years would be the best years of my life— in that, he was wrong. That was more of a statement about his life than it was about mine.

We started twice-a-day football training as soon as school began. I was told I was a fullback. However, I didn't much feel like a fullback; weren't they supposed to be great big, incredibly tough guys? It was unbearably hot on the practice field and I didn't much like the one-on-one hitting. In the second week of September, I saw a try-out announcement for the debate team. Interested, I went to the debate room where I met Dan Tewell, the coach. He gave me a copy of

Patrick Henry's "Give me liberty or give me death" speech and told me to memorize it and come back tomorrow and deliver it for him. I sweated through the memory work that night, slept poorly, and showed up in the third floor debate room first thing the next morning. Dan sat in the middle desk on the front row, told me to "do it like you mean it" and I did. When I got to the final "I know not what course others may take, but as for me, give me liberty..." I knew I had made the team. Dan congratulated me and told me about the team's meeting and travel schedule. Uh, oh! I told him that some of those times conflicted with football practice and games. He said he knew that; I couldn't be on both the football and the debate teams. It didn't take me thirty seconds to decide I'd make a better debater than I would a third-string, lightweight, sophomore fullback. It took me a lot longer to figure out how I was going to break this to my Dad.

Dad and I hadn't been on the same wave-length since I hit puberty; sometimes I wondered if we had been on the same planet. Killing his dream of having a son star in football did not improve things. That I would choose something as...(as what?)...as debate over football was incomprehensible to him. Over the next three years, he came to see me compete at track meets and even came to a debate or two, but we basically did not speak to each other throughout my high school years. He thought that debating made me arrogant and insufferable to him and Mom. While that was not my analysis at the time, I later concluded that the problem was that I was arrogant and insufferable to him and Mom.

Debate was my most important experience in high school. First, there were the debate team members. Almost to a person, they were intelligent and were from some of the best families in town. Second there was the travel. We wore suits and ties, we stayed in hotels, we ate in restaurants. Suits, hotels, and restaurants were three things with which I had almost no experience. And, Dan Tewell, bless him, did his best to teach us to be ladies and gentlemen when we dressed up, stayed in those hotels, and ate in those restaurants. Finally, there was the debate experience itself. Standing in front of a judge, we mastered our nerves, we controlled our gestures, and we spoke: "when weighed on the scales of reasoning and logic, you must agree that the affirmative side of the question...." The ability I gained on the high school debate team to speak confidently in front of an audience was one of the main factors in any success I have had.

As I grew up, I felt no pressure from my parents to go to college. As I perceived it, my Dad expected me to leave the house when I hit eighteen; my Mom thought anything I chose to do would be wonderful. Through debate and a wonderful senior English teacher, college became a distinct possibility. Miss Marsh was a teacher who lit up the English language. Poetry and prose. Shakespeare and Twain. She gave me As in her class, encouraged me to go to college, and recommended me for a job as a reporter for the *Pittsburg Sun* (our local morning newspaper). I was interviewed and hired as "deaths and funerals" editor at the Sun for $1 an hour, five nights a week, weekends off. When I wasn't writing obits, I would be allowed to study on the job. And, I reiterate, weekends off! I had two of the three things I would need to matriculate at Kansas State Teacher's College at Pittsburg: a high school diploma and a job! I needed a place to live.

After hearing that I wanted to go to college, my Dad took time to think things over. After a few days, he was ready to talk to me. He said he thought it was a good thing that I wanted to go to college. And, he wanted to help me. First, even though I was approaching my eighteenth birthday and he had expected me to be on my own by then, I could continue to live at home without charge for room and board. Second, he would help me with the $110 per semester tuition. He suggested that we take turns paying for it. He said I should take the first turn. (Obviously, if I flunked out in my first semester, he wouldn't have a turn). I accepted with true gratitude—a sign of increasing maturity.

I attended classes at Kansas State Teacher's College during the day and wrote obituaries at night. At 6 o'clock at night I would arrive at the Sun building in downtown Pittsburg, sit down at my desk and go through the stack of obits and other reporting assignments made by the night editor, Ken Hand, late of the Dallas Morning News. Ken was a short, barrel-chested, balding, fiftyish chain-smoker with a Camel-raspy voice. I can still hear him growl, "pick up" into the squawk box, ordering the linotypists to come get his edited copy for type-setting. My pre-assigned work, banged out on an antiquated black Underwood typewriter, usually lasted until about 9 p.m., at which time I began to study. Usually around 1 a.m., the paper was "put to bed" and the distribution staff down in the basemen took over. I soon learned that Ron Girotto, a friend from junior and senior high school days who was a year older than I, was the distribution manager. "Distribution manager" was a glorified name for the boss of the paper boys, much as "Deaths and Funerals Editor" was a glorified name for what I did. Our paths crossed and entwined through various stages of our lives—junior high and high schools, college, the army, Houston. Eventually, by a series of twists and turns, Ron became my chief operating officer and chief financial officer during my years at Houston's Methodist. He remains one of my very best friends and a man I respect and admire.

My first few months as a reporter under the stern eye of Ken Hand were not easy ones. I was recommended by Miss Marsh for the job because she thought I could write; Mr. Hand thought otherwise. Every time I handed in an obit or a story, it came back to me for rewriting covered in Ken's blue pencil marks. Every time. And, sometimes a piece would be sent back to me repeatedly. "Redundant." "Trite." "Clumsy." Those and more colorful notations covered my work. I did not appreciate at the time that I was learning to write. Our rocky start, and a few names I misspelled in obituaries, nearly got me fired by Christmas break. But, Ken decided to give me one more chance. I worked all four of my college years for the *Sun*. Not only was it a great learning experience and a made-to-order job for a student, they also let me take the summers off. By the time I finished my first year of college while living at home, I needed a summer to get away.

My black and white 1955 Chevy hard-top was heading straight west into the sun. Literally, straight. The road to Colorado through the wheat fields of Western Kansas aims at Denver and never deviates; the golden monotony is broken only every thirty miles by an intersection anchored by a grain elevator, a Dairy Queen, and a gas station. The open front windows made the 75 miles an hour hot, noisy, and windy. Nonetheless, as I drove alone toward the Rocky Mountains, my heart soared. This was my first real experience with freedom. It wasn't the freedom that men died for in World War II; I had always had that. It was closer to the freedom of Jack Kerouac's "On the Road," but not as beat as that. It was a nineteen-year-old-kid-out-of-his-father's-house, driving-his-own-car, leaving-a-small-town, heading-for-Denver-with-high-expectations kind of freedom.

I picked Denver for the summer because of the mountains. Plus, I had friends and relatives in the state. I didn't have a job, but thought I could get one easily. I hit Denver. My car broke down. So much for freedom and expectations. I called my Dad; he wired money. I found a room in Mrs. Leonard's house on a street just two blocks off East Colfax. I became the bellboy at the Fountain Inn, a three-story hotel/motel about three blocks from my rooming house. I worked a split shift. At six in the morning, I picked up the rolls and Danish at the bakery and took them to work, where I handled the breakfast room-service rush. I was off from 10 a.m. until 8 p.m., when I returned to handle the booze and dinner business until midnight. I learned to hate working a split shift; I learned to love the job. It is the only job I have ever had that provided immediate feedback on performance— in cash. Provide a service, get cash. Provide a service with a smile, get more cash. Provide a service with a smile and do it quickly— get much more cash. The harder I worked and the nicer I was to the customers, the more money I made! That job taught me lessons about service that would show up later in my career.

That summer of work and play in the mountains ended badly. One Sunday night in August as I was driving back to Denver following a visit to my Aunts Gladys and Edna in eastern Colorado, I began to feel sick and fatigued. I pulled the car off the highway and slept for about thirty minutes in the front seat, then drove on into Denver. I slowly dragged myself up the stairs of Mrs. Leonard's house and laid back across my bed fully-clothed with my feet still on the floor. I awoke in that same position twelve hours later—very short of breath.

At Wheatridge Hospital, the doctor said I had a mild case of viral pneumonia. It stayed mild and viral for about twenty-four hours. Then it turned serious and staphylococcal. The hospital called my folks and told them to come quickly, there wasn't much time. Days later, at some point in my fever, another close call went my way. I was in the hospital nine days. When I got out of the hospital, I immediately started the 450-mile drive back to Pittsburg, fully intending to make it in one hop. I didn't make it 150 miles before I had to stop and sleep—thirteen hours. As I drove on toward home the next day, I started counting my close calls—hit by a car, Asian flu, Whizzer wreck, double staphylococcus pneumonia. I began to hope that, like the cat, I would have nine lives. At the rate I was going, I would need at least nine.

Knowing that men my age had a military obligation, I decided to take advanced ROTC in my junior and senior years in college. If I were going to have to serve, it made sense to me to do it as an officer. As silly as it may sound, I had played "war" as long as I could remember as a kid and the idea of leading men in battle appealed to me. I took the training and the course work seriously and I did well. I was named a Cadet Battalion Commander for my senior year and was married to Betty Keith by her father, the pastor of the First Presbyterian Church.

Graduation day brought both a sheepskin and a commission in the United States Regular Army. I stood proudly in my uniform as my wife, Betty, and mother pinned on the shining gold bars of a second lieutenant of Infantry. I was a Regular officer, as opposed to a Reserve officer, because I had been named a distinguished military graduate and I had agreed to serve on active duty for three, rather than two, years. I was an Infantry officer because I chose to be. First choice of branch of service went to the distinguished military graduates in order of their class rank. Most of the choices were combat arms (infantry, armor, artillery), while places in less dangerous branches like supply, transportation, and medical service were limited. As one of the first to choose, I heard the sighs of relief of those farther down the list when I proudly took what many deemed to be an unpopular and dangerous branch. My reasoning was that the military was a potential career for me, the infantry produced the most generals, and that if I were going to go Bear, I might as well go Grizzly.

In August of 1965, Betty and I drove out of Pittsburg in a Ford Fairlane 500, pulling a U-Haul, bound for Fort Benning, Georgia, "Home of the Infantry." We drove along the lovely Gulf coast, through sleepy towns like Biloxi (before the Casinos) and angled northeast through Alabama toward

Georgia. Mile after mile, we passed Army convoys from Fort Benning heading toward the coast. At a gas station, I asked the attendant if he knew who they were and where they were going. He said, "Sure, that's the First Cavalry Division going to Vietnam."

The First Cav rolling by on its way to the docks of Mobile and points East should have been an omen to me. It wasn't. I had no concern about Vietnam; I had orders to the Berlin Brigade for my permanent assignment. I knew that a tour in Germany was for three years and that my total active duty obligation was also three years. I was profoundly wrong on both counts.

The Infantry Officers' Basic Course was designed to immerse young officers in the culture of the foot soldier; to change soft college boys into men who were physically and mentally tough enough to lead others into battle. We were schooled on rifle, mortar, artillery, and grenade ranges; we called in artillery fire and air strikes; we practiced radio communications; but, most importantly, we began to understand and accept the responsibilities and gravity of leadership on the field of battle. We learned to carry ourselves with pride and crisp military bearing. We learned to "walk with a purpose" and to "do something, even if it's wrong." At the end of six weeks, we had been toughened.

"Airborne." The word rang out from men as they saluted officers who wore the red glider patch of the paratroopers. Fort Benning was also the Army's parachute training center. For three weeks following the basic course, I ran, performed the "Army Daily Dozen" exercises, practiced parachute landing falls, jumped from the 32 foot and the 200 foot towers in preparation for the real thing: exiting a perfectly good aircraft in fright. Paratrooper training is egalitarian. Lieutenants, Captains, Majors, non-commissioned officers and enlisted men were trained in ranks together with no differentiation—we were all just "troops." As we bounced around in the bay of the C130 plane, on the way to the drop zone for our first jump, the fear was palpable. It was stiflingly hot in the bay; many of the men had never flown before, some vomited and the acrid stench made the strongest stomachs turn. There were pale faces and white eyes all around. The jumpmaster opened the door and outside air mercifully rushed over us. "Stand Up." "Hook Up." The standard set of commands ended with the ultimate one: "GO." I ran to the door in the side of the C130 and dove out—1,000 feet above the red dirt of the Old South. And, into the roaring whirlwind of the prop blast. "One thousand one, one thousand two, one thousand three I counted (eyes closed I prayed to God: please let it open at four) one thousand four." G force on my body, the sound of the chute billowing open, then complete silence. I looked up at the snowy canopy above me, down at the drop zone, and out at the horizon. This was so serene and peaceful. It lasted for forty-five seconds. I clobbered into the plowed earth at 22 miles an hour. Four qualifying jumps later, I proudly pinned on the silver wings of the paratrooper.

Berlin, the former Nazi capital, was an occupied city when I arrived in November, 1965. The four powers—United States, Britain, France, and Russia—had divided it into sectors. Most of the eastern part of Berlin was in the Russian sector, and when citizens there started leaving that sector in droves, the Russians hit upon a concrete, stone, and barbed wire solution. The Berlin Wall had gone up just a few years before I arrived and tensions were still high.

I was assigned as a platoon leader in a rifle company in one of the battalions of the Sixth Infantry, an honored and historic unit. I loved the job and the men. Among other duties, my platoon was assigned for a week as military guard for Spandau Prison. The prison had only three prisoners, but what a threesome: Baldur Von Shirach, former Hitler Youth Leader,

Albert Speer, former Minister of Armaments, and Rudolph Hess, former Deputy Fuehrer of the Third Reich. As officer of the guard, I would walk through the prison garden while the three took their exercise. The extraordinary garden was the product of the labor of the three men for twenty years. It was about 100 x 50 feet in size, was crisscrossed in brick paths they had meticulously laid, and contained beautifully and lovingly maintained flowerbeds, plants, shrubs, and pools. Speer and Von Shirach would walk there together, not talking, while Hess, head down and mumbling to himself, paced on the other side of the garden. Though forbidden to speak to the prisoners, one morning I couldn't resist: "Guten morgen, Herr Speer." The reply came in the crispest British-accented English and with such good cheer, "Why good morning to you, too, Lieutenant." That was startling. How could that much evil be packaged in such charm? Another of life's lessons!

On a cold and rainy night in October of 1966, while I watched on television from our quarters, Speer and Von Schirach were released from Spandau. They had served their twenty-year sentences. They left behind an immense prison for just one prisoner —a lone, deranged, old Nazi whose sentence was for life.

Halfway through my Berlin tour of duty, I was handed official orders to leave within 30 days for the Military Advisor's course at Fort Bragg, North Carolina, and upon completion, to proceed immediately to the Republic of Vietnam.

That changed everything. From a European adventure as an officer and gentleman to the deadliness of war. Those orders brought me to a previously unknown sharp focus on the important things in life. When I told a fellow officer that I had orders for Vietnam, the look on his face said "death sentence." The look on my pregnant wife's was indescribable.

We left Europe and returned to Pittsburg. Our plan was

for me to go through the Fort Bragg training, which would end in late May, then take a 30-day leave so that I would have a month at home with mother and new baby. It was a good plan, but as with so many good plans, it didn't work out that way.

Off I went to learn to be a Military Advisor to the Vietnamese Infantry. The training at Fort Bragg was deadly earnest. All of us officers knew we were going into combat—and, soon. We worked hard on our Vietnamese language skills, learning sophisticated communications like "first company go left." The language is tonal. The same word said with six different inflections means six different things—often very unrelated things. The wrong inflection might change "lady" to "hog." Unfortunately, I am almost tone deaf; I mastered little Vietnamese. We worked on our physical conditioning, pressed on by Korean War veterans' stories of infantry companies overrun because of poor conditioning. Weapons training had never held our concentration as it did.

We desperately hoped that our baby would be born while I was on leave in Pittsburg. But as each day went by and no baby appeared, both Betty and I were beginning to get panicky. We implored the doctor to do something; he prescribed castor oil. Contractions began and stopped just as we reached the labor room at Mt. Carmel hospital. After thirty-six hours, I stood outside of the delivery room and looked through a window as the doctor took forceps and, using all his strength, extracted a baby girl. Betty had neither moaned nor cried during all those hours of labor, but when the forceps were applied, she screamed. I will remember that single scream as long as I have memory.

Julie Elizabeth Mathis was eleven days old when I put on my formal uniform—dress blues with gold epaulettes—and posed with her in our front yard for what, I wondered, might be the only pictures ever taken of this father and daughter. The next morning I left for Vietnam.

At 0200 hours, the Reconnaissance Platoon started to move down the dirt road and into Phu Hoa Dong. It was so dark that I had to stay within an arm's length of the small Vietnamese soldier in front of me to follow the column. I was in the middle of the file, with Sergeant Mitchell—one of our advisory team members—behind me. We moved off the road and began to snake among the houses of the sleeping peasants. The operation was designed to take this Viet Cong-sympathizing village away from the enemy. Three battalions of American infantry had moved into blocking positions to the east, while three battalions of Vietnamese infantry blocked from the west. Phu Hoa Dong was surrounded. The platoon's mission was to find the Viet Cong and force them out of the village and into the blocking positions. Suddenly, the column stopped; everyone went down on one knee. I turned back to speak to Mitch—he wasn't there. Sergeant Mitchell and half the platoon were gone. I was the last man in the line. My first combat operation with the First Battalion, Seventh Regiment, of the Fifth Division of the Army of the Republic of Vietnam (ARVN) was not going well.

Ten days earlier, I had left home for San Francisco, where in Haight-Ashbury I got a brief preview of what America was about to go through. I caught my assigned 707 and we started to hop across the Pacific. After a grueling twenty-two hours, we approached the coastline of Vietnam. Sitting in a window seat in a comfortable commercial airliner, watching flares float to the ground in the dark over a combat zone, was a major psychological disconnect. Was this any way to go to war? We landed at Tan Son Nhut, the mammoth U.S Air Force base outside of Saigon, where we were processed into the country and given our unit assignments. I was joining a unit that previously had been decimated. The Seventh Regiment had been overrun by North Vietnamese regulars in the rubber trees of the Michelin plantation. Rebuilt and retrained, it was taking the field again in an area north of Saigon, near Cu Chi. My battalion was assigned a key role in taking Phu Hoa Dong, a village just across the Saigon River from an area known, because of heavy enemy concentration, as the Iron Triangle. Once taken, the town was to be occupied as a base of combat operations by the First Battalion. Phu Hoa Dong would be my home base for seven months.

The fighting that occurred in the occupation of the village was sporadic—nothing like the pitched battle we had expected. On the first night of the operation, the platoon did not make contact with the enemy as it pushed through the village. That was lucky. Sgt. Mitchell had lost sight of me in the moonless night and wandered away, at the head of a new column, on his own path toward our objective at the other end of the hamlet. With him went our radio—my only way to call in artillery and air strikes. Had we hit the Viet Cong divided, we could have been mauled; had the divided columns bumped into each other in the dark, we could have had a disaster.

After three days, the operation ended. Phu Hoa Dong was "secured." The First Battalion began clearing the western side of the village and constructing three defensive compounds, the main one in the center, with company-sized outposts to the north and south. For forty days, as bunkers were sandbagged and fields of fire were cleared for mutual support among the compounds, we conducted small unit patrols and ambushes along the stream banks and in the rice paddies that surrounded the town. For forty nights, I slipped between two green sheets of nylon, sewn together into a light hammock tied between two trees, and slept. I slept so soundly that, on several occasions, I snored through incoming mortar and rifle grenade rounds.

When the construction was complete, we moved into our new bunker in the center of the middle compound. It was about twenty feet long and eight feet wide. Its walls were made of sandbags which had been pounded into rough, blocked rectangles for better fit. The roof, which later became the home for a family of mice and a snake of some kind, was a series of logs laid across the walls and topped with a double layer of sandbags. Gun ports were built into the walls and covered with steel mesh wire to prevent grenades from being tossed in on us. Our four-man advisory team moved cots in and strung up mosquito nets. Near the bunker was the mess tent where our Chinese cook/body guard, Chuan, presided. One day, Chuan hung a whole, feathered chicken by the neck at the ridge pole of the tent.. He kept it there in the magnified tropical heat under the canvas until the chicken's head separated from its body and it dropped to the ground. He cooked it; we ate it. When it was time for a shower, we stood naked outside of our bunker on a wooden pallet set beside a fifty-five gallon barrel filled with sun-warmed water and used a one-gallon can to pour it over us. Our lives there were mostly uneventful. By day, we slept, played cards, or drove—wearing our black Viet Cong "pajamas"—into the center of the village for soup and beer. By night, we accompanied ten-man ambush teams out into the countryside.

The average American foot-soldier in Vietnam feared the Viet Cong, mines, and American artillery—in reverse order. I shared the fear of the foot soldier. The Viet Cong were laying low around Phu Hoa Dong, with only an occasional sniper round or mortar shell to remind us of their presence. Mines are nasty little surprises that can tear your guts out, take your legs off, or leave you bleeding and dying in the dirt, but they usually only hit one or two men. American artillery is awesome in its destructive power, and when accidentally rained in on friendly troops, it can decimate whole units, killing and maiming scores. News reports often refer to "friendly fire," meaning bullets and artillery shells fired at a unit by other units of the same army. Trust me on this, there is no "friendly fire!" And what a futile and pathetic way to die—

killed by accident by your own people.

It was early evening during the rainy season. The monsoon had come through in late afternoon and had left the compound cleansed. I was not scheduled for a patrol that night, so I took a shower, put on a clean pair of black pajamas and climbed up on the roof of our bunker to enjoy the evening. Without warning, four 155-millimeter artillery shells burst in the air over my head. Shrapnel was everywhere. The smell of cordite and the cries of the wounded assaulted the senses. I flipped backward off the roof and dove into the bunker, grabbed the radio handset and screamed into the mouthpiece, "Savage Four Niner, this is Leroy Almond Two Zero, Cease Fire! Cease Fire!" I raged at the U.S. 25th Infantry's Division Artillery in Cu Chi, telling the radio operator at the other end who and where we were. After several minutes, he apologized and explained that they were firing harassing and interdicting missions and had not updated their maps to include ARVN unit locations. One dead and seven wounded in the first battalion— from "friendly fire." I, fully exposed under the blasts, did not receive a scratch. Another close call. Another of my nine lives gone?

I stayed in Phu Hoa Dong for my entire seven months in the field. It was a relatively quiet time there because, as we were soon to learn, the enemy had been busy preparing for something big. I was transferred to Fifth Division headquarters at Lam Son to become, briefly, our division's liaison officer to the First U.S. Infantry Division—The Big Red One—at Lai Khe. Every day, I would catch a chopper to Lai Khe in time for the afternoon briefing on the operations being conducted by the First Infantry, spend the night, then chopper back to Lam Son to brief Fifth ARVN's senior officers. Eighteen days after coming in from the field, the Battle of Tet began for me in a terrifying rain of mortar rounds and 122-millimeter Soviet rockets on the Big Red One headquarters. For days, Lai Khe was under fire. I would fly into the hot landing zone, walk or catch a lift on a passing jeep to the HQ while the shells impacted, do my job, find a hole to sleep in, and dash out early the next morning to catch a ride back to my division. I learned that my old unit had been hard hit in the battle. A reinforced North Vietnamese Regiment (three times the size of the First battalion), attacked the compounds on the west side of Phu Hoa Dong. The captain who had replaced me as senior advisor and his new assistant were both killed. So was Sgt. Rex Freeman, who had been with me in the battalion from the beginning.

After the battle of Tet and my seven months of leadership in a combat unit, I had a changed view of life. I had learned that leadership in life and death situations is different than that described in the management books. The relationship between a combat leader and his men is more serious and more fragile. It requires a unique degree of faith and trust—flowing both ways. Until my tour in Vietnam, I had taken life for granted, accepting whatever came on its own terms. Now, I knew that life was a gift bestowed randomly. If I were to be one of the lucky recipients, there were obligations. As one given the ability to lead, I had the sacred obligation to be the best leader possible. I had the obligation to appreciate life itself—every day. And, I was obligated to do something with it—something serious, something important.

Dear Mr. President:

As required by law, I hereby submit my resignation from the Regular Army of the United States of America to be effective with the completion of my third year of active duty, 26 August 1968.

I signed it Captain Mathis.

During my months in combat I had done a lot of thinking; I had come to some conclusions about my future. My first conclusion: I did not want a career in the military. While I was proud to wear the uniform and proud of my war service, I was disgusted with the way the war was fought. The U.S. Army was hampered by political, military, and geographic restraints. America was asking its young men to die fighting with their hands tied behind their backs. Our side never lost a battle involving a company-sized or larger unit; but, as a North Vietnamese delegate to the Paris peace talks observed, "that was irrelevant." America was beaten politically. It had the stomach to send its kids to war, but not the heart to bring them home winners.

It did not take the Department of the Army long to respond. The answer was in my hands in two weeks. Perhaps, it noted, I was unaware of something called the "Selective Officer Retention Act" in which, for the good of the country in times of national crisis (which these were), selected officers (which I was), could be retained on active duty. "Therefore, Captain Mathis, you are hereby selectively retained on active duty as a Regular Officer for a period of twenty-four additional months." TWO MORE YEARS!

The second conclusion I had reached: I wanted to go to Washington University in St. Louis and earn a master's degree in hospital administration. Now, three years out of college with a wife and child, I needed a professional education that could be gotten quickly (on campus work at Washington University was just three semesters) and produced income soonest (the degree included a paid residency). After the war, I needed a profession, too, that did good.

The worst part of the two-year extension was the prospect of a second tour in Vietnam. I indicated on my post-Vietnam assignment preference sheet that I requested duty with a division on either the east or west coast of the United States.

The orders came: ROTC duty at Washington University in St. Louis!

It seemed an eternity as the jet taxied and then stood—

waiting before take-off. As we lumbered down the runway all I could think was what an ironic waste it would be to be shot down now, in a commercial jet, after all that combat. As the Boeing 707 leveled out above mortar and rocket range, over the South China Sea and away from the coastline of South Vietnam, the tension began to ebb from my body. My thoughts turned to my new assignment. Phenomenal coincidence? What else could it be? Not only was it an assignment smack in the middle of the country, as far away from either coast as it could be, it was a teaching job at a university I planned to attend—not a troop command. It was precisely what I wanted and, because of that, I would never have thought to request it. And, best of all, it was a two-year stabilized assignment. That meant no more Vietnam for me! I reclined my seat, kicked off my shoes. I was coming home.

In uniform, with rows of medals, wearing the paratrooper cap, I walked beside the major as we entered the impressive quadrangle of Washington University. It was my orientation tour as a new professor of military science. As we crossed the stately quad, I glanced up into a nearby tree. There, in the low branches, sat a young man and two young women—naked. They were smoking pot.

I had come home to an America changed—one I did not know. When I left campus for the Army in 1965, fraternity men wore shirts and ties on Tuesdays. Their haircuts were short and neat. A demonstration was a method of instruction. A keg party was our mind-altering experience. From there, I entered the insular world of the military. I spent most of my time on Army posts, many of which were overseas, where news and information were carefully managed. In three short years, America became a strange and different place to me. During my two years as an ROTC instructor on a liberal university campus, I was vilified, cursed, and spat at by angry young people with long hair and bad grooming, because I wore the uniform of the forces that guaranteed their freedom to do so. Having just risked my life for a year at the request of my country, I found myself in a greater state of culture shock in Missouri than I had experienced in either Germany or Vietnam.

It wasn't just the flower children, the demonstrations against the war, or the kids on psychedelic drugs, it was also the change of pace. I had spent the last twelve months totally immersed in my work (that's one way of putting it). ROTC duty was not as demanding. I was assigned to teach senior cadets infantry small unit tactics.

When I wasn't doing that, or preparing lesson plans, I was free to do other things. I played handball most mornings; I played golf twice a week. We not only had our military leave days, we took all school holidays off as well. I used the unaccustomed extra time to learn to be a husband again, to be a father for the first time, and to make improvements to the home we had purchased. We took long driving vacations; we camped and canoed. All of this normal life was disconcerting and amazing; how could this much normalcy exist at the same time friends were fighting and dying in a war I had just left behind? Juxtaposed to the serenity of my suburban idyll were the constant ugly demonstrations and protests by the SDS (Students for a Democratic Society), which demanded the removal of ROTC from the Washington University campus.

The call came at midnight. I quickly threw on a pair of jeans and a sweatshirt, got into the VW bug and drove fast across south St. Louis toward the campus. As I neared the corner where the ROTC offices squatted near the gymnasium, I saw the trucks and the red glow against the dark trees. I got out of the car and joined the small group officers who were silently watching their offices burn. Failing to convince the university administration to remove the blight of ROTC from the peace-loving campus, the SDS took matters into its own hands. We had seen it coming. Day after day, the protesters came. They pounded on the windows of the classrooms to disrupt our classes, shouting slogans. They disrupted drill formations on the practice field, draping cadets with flowers. At one protest, a young coed became so caught up in the moment that she decided to remove her blouse and bra, thereby publicly dedicating a lovely set of breasts to the anti-war effort. Seven times, they tried to bomb or burn our building. On this, the seventh, they burned it to the ground.

But, the war was never far below the surface of our now more tranquil lives. It periodically reared its bloody head. ROTC officers served as notification officers for the families of officers and men missing or killed in action. In uniform, I went to mansions in LaDue, slums on the near west side, and blue-collar neighborhoods by the Busch brewery to deliver the devastating news. Death was not class conscious; it did not discriminate on any basis. It was not fair; it was not just. Its random touch brought pain and sorrow with no regard to the good, the bad, the worthy, the unworthy. Through me, its grim tidings came to the poor, the white, the wealthy, the black, and the middle-class. Mothers, seeing me come up the walk in uniform, would burst into tears, collapse, or watch dry-eyed and severe, their only hope that he was missing and not killed—a hope rarely rewarded.

On September 5, 1970, after five years in the Army—at war both at home and abroad—I concluded another major segment of my life by processing out of the service. While I had agreed to serve only three years, I did not begrudge the extra two years I contributed to my country. I wore the uniform with pride then and it is with pride that I now assess those years. They were years that brought me life and death challenges far earlier than anyone should have to face them; they were years that taught me the consequences of bad leadership and the sheer joy of good leadership; and they were years that only recently have been appreciated by the citizens of my country. A few days later, I entered the graduate program in hospital administration at the medical school—just across Forest Park from the main campus, but a world apart.

Dr. Jim Hepner, the hospital administration program's director, greeted the twenty-eight new aspiring hospital executives. We averaged 28 years of age, were predominately white, men, and veterans. Many of us were smokers. So were some of the faculty members. We wore coats and ties to class. Most of us had been out of school for several years and wondered how we would handle graduate school. Jim and his team immediately put the pressure on. The reading load was impossible, statistics incomprehensible. Demands were tough, stress high, sleep limited.

While academics were important to us, the administrative residency and subsequent jobs were the topics of constant conversation. The residency was where graduate education met the real world of the hospital—our future professional home. It meant being on a payroll again. It led to jobs. Classmates speculated on which big institutions would offer positions and which of us would land them. I was not a part of that speculation. Mine was an easy choice. We had lived in St. Louis for two years and we liked it. I planned to stay in St. Louis. I would interview for a position at Barnes, Jewish, and St. John's hospitals, all local. I was sure I would be accepted at one of them. Like so many of my plans, it was not to be.

"Dr. and Mrs. Hepner would like for you and Mrs. Mathis to join them at their home for dinner tomorrow night." The program secretary's message was as unusual as it was unexpected. With the requisite degree of nervousness, my wife and I rang the doorbell of the Hepner's impressive home. After a gracious dinner, we got the full court press. Houston's Methodist Hospital—"The Methodist Hospital"—was a long-time residency site for the Washington University program.

Jim wanted to be sure someone who would fit the culture there and would do well filled that residency slot. It was important to the school. Would I interview there? I thanked the Hepners for a lovely evening and for their confidence in me. I promised to seriously consider it and would let them know soon.

Well, that threw a wrench in the works! Betty and I talked it over; pro and con. We didn't want to leave our home. Barnes, Jewish, and St. John's were first rate. But, Houston was a bigger place. We had driven through Houston on the way to a Gulf beach vacation and had liked the look of it. Methodist was the home of world famous surgeon, Dr. Michael DeBakey. Finally, on the con side, I didn't have the money for plane fare to get there for an interview. That decided it. I would tell the Hepners "no."

Days later, I came home from class, grabbed the mail from the box on the front porch, went down the steps to the basement, and flopped down on the couch in my study. I flipped through the usual assortment of bills and magazines, but stopped at a fat envelope with a First Presbyterian Church, Pittsburg, Kansas, return address. I opened it and stared at the note and the plane tickets. My father-in-law thought that an opportunity as good as Methodist should be explored. He had sent tickets for Houston. It was another of those out-of-the-blue strange interventions in the direction of my life. First, the phenomenal coincidence of the Army sending me to Washington University, now another unexpected external nudge. This time to Methodist. It wouldn't be the last strange intervention.

I began my administrative residence in August of 1971. I had not met Methodist's administrator, Ted Bowen, during the interview process. But I knew all about him. He was one of the big names in the field. As I shook his hand on that first day of residency, I was impressed. Here was the legendary hospital administrator who had showcased and supported Dr.

Michael DeBakey; whose hospital was chosen by the Duke of Windsor for his surgery; whose institution was the site of so many of the early heart transplants. We liked each other immediately.

During my first week I was assigned to Mr. Bowen as a prelude to rotating through the departments. He invited me to join him at a breakfast meeting. There were four people at the meeting: Mr. Bowen, Dr. DeBakey, former Texas Governor John Connally—and me! I do not remember the subject of the meeting; I do remember the heady sensation of being included in such an intimate and august group. I knew what was to come in the weeks, months, and years ahead would be incredible.

The nine-month residency was early mornings, late nights. It included shadowing Mr. Bowen wherever he went, extensive writing and project work for him, and even a week in our cardiovascular operating rooms, where I learned to revere and respect physicians. It also included escorting VIP guests throughout our complex. King Leopold of Belgium was more interesting than most; on tour, when we took the elevator, every time the door opened, the King would try to get off. "I'm sorry, Sir, this is not our floor," I told him. He looked somewhat bemused. As a King, he was accustomed to elevators opening only at his destination. With little more than a month to completion of the residency, Mr. Bowen asked me what I wanted to do when it was over. I might have tried being coy; I could have been more sophisticated. I was neither as I blurted, "I want to work for you, Mr. Bowen."

A good job with an excellent salary and benefits brought the expected results. We bought a new home and decided to complete our family. On the morning of the seventh of March, 1973, I brought Betty to Methodist where she walked comfortably onto the obstetrics floor, was anesthetized and induced, and gave birth to Jennifer Leigh Mathis. At that time,

Methodist did not permit fathers in the delivery room, so I spent my time waiting in my office. When birth was imminent, the nurses called me to the third floor. I held that pink bundle in my arms and marveled at the new life. When the nurses took Jennifer to the bassinet, I thought of six-year-old Julie and wondered how she would react to having a little sister—better, I hoped, than I had when I was six and my sister collided with my world.

Vice President! At 31!

Then came the strange death of Howard Hughes as he tried to reach Methodist for medical care and the flood of The Methodist Hospital. Mr. Bowen received a call from out-of-state notifying him that the reclusive Texas billionaire, Howard Hughes, was in critical condition and in route by private jet to Houston for medical treatment. The caller urged strictest confidentiality. Mr. Bowen immediately called Dr. DeBakey and the two went to the surgical intensive care unit to arrange for a highly confidential patient. I was put in charge of the administrative component of a medical and administrative team to meet the plane, clear customs (Hughes was coming in from Acapulco, Mexico) and get the patient to Methodist. Our small, nervous group stood sweating amid an ambulance and several station wagons on the hot airport concrete as we watched the Lear jet land and taxi slowly toward us. The plane stopped and we gathered around the door. It opened. Inside lay the emaciated body of Howard Hughes, oxygen mask still covering his mouth. An accompanying physician told us he had died as the plane touched down. What now? Dr. McIntosh, the head of the medical team, decided we should take the body back to Methodist for post-mortem examination. It would have been wiser, in retrospect, to call the county medical examiner then and there and let him deal with the situation. We didn't. We took the body of Howard Hughes to the morgue at the hospital and began the strange circus that attended his death.

As soon as I reached the hospital, the director of Public Relations pounced on me. CBS was sending a camera crew to Methodist for an interview about Howard Hughes. NBC was calling. UPI was trying to confirm the rumor that Hughes was a patient at the hospital. Local radio and television stations were descending upon us. The Houston Chronicle and the Post had reporters in the Public Relations offices. We were in the midst of a media feeding frenzy—before I had heard that term or knew what one was. I told her to hold the arriving press in the hospital's assembly room; I would be there as soon as I had something I could tell them. After a series of consultations with the doctors accompanying Hughes, the medical examiner, the Houston cousin who was next of kin, the hospital was ready to release to the world the news about Howard Hughes. I was designated to deliver it. At 6:30 p.m., on April 5, 1976, I walked in a side door of the hospital's assembly room and was immediately blinded by banks and banks of camera lights. The room was tightly packed. I moved to the lectern. Microphones from the national and local radio and television reporters had covered it. What I had to say was brief and we had decided I would take no questions. I steeled myself to speak clearly and confidently (it wasn't easy): "Today at 1:27 p.m., while en route from Acapulco to Houston by air, Mr. Howard R. Hughes expired. Mr. Hughes was in route to The Methodist Hospital for medical treatment. Additional information can be obtained by contacting...." As I concluded, I turned on my heels and headed briskly toward the door. Almost as a single shout, the assembled reporters yelled, "WAIT." Taken aback, I paused. The next shout was, "Who are you?" I had not even thought to identify myself. I went back to the lectern, gave my name and title, then left. Thus, did I announce to the world the death of Howard Robards Hughes.

The Neurosensory Center of Houston was under

construction in the summer of 1976 when the rain started. What was to become the home of three of Methodist's medical services—Ophthalmology, Otorhinolaryngology, and Neurology—was a three-story deep, one city block square pit next to Methodist's cardiovascular and orthopedic facility, the Fondren/Brown Building. From the pit, the contractor had punched openings into the building at the basement and sub-basement levels for connecting walkways and utility chases. Record setting rain started in the early afternoon. Houston is flat and poorly drained. Normal rains can bring the city's traffic to a halt: storm sewers overflow and the water rises in the streets. The executives at Methodist were used to Houston in the rain. Methodist had never flooded; no Texas Medical Center institution had. None of us gave any thought to the huge open pit on the north end of our campus.

It rained. And, rained. A straight downpour, never slaking, hour after hour. At six o'clock in the evening, the call came into the executive offices from the communications department. "There is water in the Fondren/Brown basement and in the switchboard area." Several of us ran down the stairs of the Main Building and into the tunnel connecting it to Fondren/Brown. As I entered the building, I stopped dumbstruck. Water was pouring up out of the elevator shafts. It quickly rose to a foot of water, then two. I looked down the hall through the window in the door into communications. The operators had barricaded themselves in the department. I led a team to get them out—the water was rising rapidly and I didn't know how high it might go. We tried to get the door opened. It swung toward the rapidly building wall of water. It wouldn't budge. Finally, with the water at three feet, we gave a great pull and it opened, sending a small tidal wave into the communications department, knocking over chairs and several of the operators. Just then, as we were helping the drenched communications staff out of their ruined department, the lights flickered once, twice, and then went out. I heard the backup generators kick in. Then they died. They were in the sub-basement of the building, completely under water.

There is no adequate way to describe how I felt as I watched the lights go out in a modern, 1000-bed hospital. Helpless. Stunned. Fearful. My thoughts went immediately to the third-floor cardiovascular operating rooms and intensive care unit. I hoped that all of the surgeries had been completed by this time of day, but what of the 50 patients in ICU, many on electrical devices including ventilators? What on earth do we do now?

In retrospect, it is easy to understand what happened. As the rainwater in the streets rose, it began to pour into the construction pit in a tremendous three-sided waterfall. As it filled, water entered the sub-basement chases and walkways that had been cut into the adjacent Fondren/Brown building, then through existing chases and walkways to the sub-basement of the Main building. When the water hit the electrical vault, city power was lost. The emergency generators kicked in as designed, but died immediately as they were completely submerged in the sub-basements. The generators, all air handling equipment, and hundreds of other electric motors were irretrievably lost. The water rose into the next level and wiped out several departments, storage areas, and research laboratories. When the rain finally stopped around midnight, the sky cleared, stars came out. Below, without electricity, air conditioning, or safe water, The Methodist Hospital stood silent and dark.

An incredible seven-day, around-the-clock effort brought Methodist back to life. In that period, city fire trucks pumped the water out, generators on semi-trailers were brought in, wiring and switches were dried and cleaned, generators were replaced (and relocated to the first floor), and hundreds of small motors and air handlers were rehabilitated and put back in service. The administrative team, the physicians, the hospital staff never were closer nor more effective than in that time of crisis. And, what of the patients? Surgery was not finished in the cardiovascular suite. A case was in progress; the chest cavity open when the lights went out. It was finished by flashlight. In ICU, the nurses manually operated the ventilators. The patients were unbelievably patient as the employees, day after day, climbed as high as ten floors to deliver bottled water and sandwiches. Not one patient died as a result of that catastrophe.

Senior Vice President at 34!

Ted Bowen's heart attack brought significant changes in the organization. The subsequent course of the disease, including by-pass surgery by Dr. DeBakey, left the team destabilized and uncertain. Mr. Bowen's decisive style and personal interaction with all executives were effective as long as he was present. When he was ill, nothing significant was accomplished. Recognizing the problem, he reorganized the executive team to include a new layer of responsible senior management. He divided the organization into three functional areas: Financial Services, Nursing Services, and Ancillary Services. A senior vice president headed each. I was named senior VP and assigned to lead Ancillary Services, which I quickly nicknamed the Third Division.

The division was a significant operating responsibility. It contained the big revenue generating services of radiology, pathology, and pharmacy; with the exception of surgery, all of Methodist's clinical services and related entities; and the main staff departments including human resources and public affairs. The executive team included, among others, vice president's Ronald G. Girotto, M. James Henderson, and Michael V. Williamson. Ron, Jim, and Mike stayed with me as key Methodist executives until my retirement nineteen years later. As a team, our challenge was difficult. First, we had to learn to work together rather than for Mr. Bowen. Because departmental budgets had always been handed down from finance (sometimes months late and well into the budget year), we had to create our own bottom-up expense and capital budgeting process. There was no divisional accounting and reporting system, so we created one. And, we all had to cope with the uncertainty and speculation surrounding an impaired president. The team developed real esprit-de-corps, a visible pride in working in the Third Division, and significantly improved the operations and financial performance of its units. Unfortunately, financial storm clouds were gathering elsewhere.

Before the financial storm broke, another Houston downpour threatened The Methodist Hospital. In April of 1979, record-breaking rain again fell. I was at home when the administrator-on-call phoned to say that hospital engineers were predicting another flood. I went cold inside. I could still clearly see that flooded, dark hospital under that starry sky three years earlier. I quickly put on some jeans, a pair of tennis shoes, and a rain jacket made out of an army rubber poncho, got in my station wagon and pulled out onto my street, which was already curb-full of running water. The water got steadily deeper as I headed south toward the Texas Medical Center. Before I had gone a mile, I knew the car was not going to make it. I pulled into a bank parking lot, which was higher than the street, locked the car, and started walking toward the hospital. Before long, I was wading. When I reached the freeway—the halfway point—and waded under it, the water reached my chest. I held my wallet above my head as I emerged onto the higher ground of a Texaco station on the south side of the freeway. As I rested for a moment, I watched a man in a canoe paddle from submerged car to submerged car. He was looking for people who might be stranded. He paddled toward the Texaco station.

"Where did you get that canoe?" I hollered at him.

"Over there. I own the canoe rental place on the other side of the freeway," he responded.

"Guess what," I said. "I would like to rent a canoe."

As I set out, the current was flowing south down the street toward Rice University and the Texas Medical Center. It was an eerie trip. Submerged cars were everywhere, some with their lights still on under the water. Plastic bags of garbage and other strange debris floated with the current along side my canoe. At University Boulevard, I turned the canoe toward the hospital and paddled harder. Trees arching over the street created a dark tunnel; I strained to see the hospital's lights. Ominously, I could see none at the end of the street. Suddenly, about twenty feet in front of the canoe, I saw a young man wading toward Methodist in the thigh-deep water. "Care to ride?" He jumped into the front seat and I handed him a paddle. As we neared Main Street, we could see cars in front of the hospital in the high water. And, we heard the roar! Methodist's new professional office building was under construction—it was a two-story-deep pit like the Neurosensory Center had been during the flood of 1976. The sound was the street water cascading into the hole. I had two immediate concerns. I didn't want to get swept into the pit and I didn't want to get hit by some barreling pickup truck as we crossed Fannin Street. Over the roar, I shouted to my now frightened companion, "When I say paddle, paddle!" As we crossed Main Street and neared the construction site, the current increased in speed and turned wickedly to the right. "Paddle, PADDLE, damn it!" We powered by the plunging water, missing the fall into the construction site by ten feet, knifed across Fannin Street without being run over, and ground to a halt in the Methodist volunteers' parking lot. I looked up. Gloriously, lights shown in windows in all the buildings. Thankfully, my wet expedition had been unnecessary. When the Houston Chronicle ran a story on the episode the following weekend, it became part of the lore of Methodist's "can do" culture.

The financial storm grew out of The Neurosensory Center, a project of both Methodist and its medical school partner, Baylor College of Medicine. The hospital and the school had launched a joint fundraising campaign, which had obtained pledges to underwrite its entire $34,000,000 construction cost. That was the good news! The bad news was that it needed to be equipped, furnished, and staffed. There was no financing plan for those costs or for the natural lag times in pledge payments. And, Mr. Bowen had a "no debt" policy. The cash demands for capital equipment, furnishings, and startup costs inundated the senior vice president for finance. He did the best he could: he delayed payments to vendors by as much as nine months; he borrowed all existing restricted funds; and unfortunately, he also stopped funding the malpractice trust fund for two years. It wasn't enough. The board had to authorize borrowing $3,000,000 to meet the hospital's payroll. Mr. Bowen—embarrassed—reassigned to other duties his longtime, loyal executive vice president and senior vice president for finance. After a brief, two-year stint as a freshly-minted Senior Vice President, he asked me to serve in the newly created position of executive vice president and chief operating officer. With alacrity, I accepted.

I was 36 years old when I was named executive vice president and chief operating officer. Most of the hospital's executives were older than I and most had worked there much longer than I had. I was overly full of myself at being named the second ranking executive at Methodist; that had its obvious minuses, of course, but it also had its plusses. The plusses were: I was confident that I knew exactly what needed to be done and I had the energy and fire in the belly to do it. I first assembled my team from the ranks of the Third Division, with

Ron Girotto as my senior vice president and chief financial officer, and Mike Williamson and Jim Henderson as senior vice presidents and division heads. Then I ordered airline tickets for Ron and me to head to Boston and Baltimore.

At that time, the Massachusetts General Hospital in Boston and the Johns Hopkins Hospital in Baltimore were thought to be the leading hospitals in the nation. I wanted us to see the perceived leaders so that we could evaluate how Methodist stacked up. After the visits, we knew we could be better. On the plane ride from Baltimore home to Houston, we agreed on our plan to fix operations and finance at Methodist.

The plan was very simple. Reorganize operations. Create a stronger finance division. Enhance revenue. Rein in operating expenses. Control capital expenses. Manage cash. Back at work, we created detailed plans for each element and began to work to make things happen. As we did, I got a small dose of humility.

Tony's restaurant in Houston is one of the fine restaurants of the world. Margaret Williamson, Mike's wife, used it frequently for their entertainment of physicians. I told her I was going to be entertaining a relative and she wholeheartedly recommended Tony's. But, she said: "Larry, be sure they know who you are when you make reservations."

"Why?" I asked.

"Because, they give the best tables to the most important people."

I went to my office, asked my secretary, Millie, to make reservations for four people for eight o'clock Saturday night at Tony's. And, I said, "Please be sure to tell them who I am Millie." Later. I asked if she had made the reservation.

"Yes. I did," she replied.

"For four at eight o'clock Saturday night?"

"Yes," she said.

"Did you tell them who I was—Executive Vice President at Methodist?"

"Yes, I did."

"What did they say?"

"They said, 'Tell him to wear a tie, '" she deadpanned.

Slowly, the new executive team began working our way out of the $20,000,000 financial hole we inherited. The price increases brought in much needed cash; the expense and capital restraints began to take hold. Ron called all the major vendors to a meeting in the auditorium of the Neurosensory Center: He needed to buy time for us to pay our sadly delinquent bills. Fortunately, they agreed. The cash management plan began working. Within six months of assuming our new executive positions, we could see that our rescue plan would work. Within twelve months, we were again current on payables and had retired the $3,000,000 bank loan. In 18 months, we had fully refunded the malpractice trust fund and, at the two-year mark, we completed the recovery by fully repaying the ransacked restricted funds. The hospital's operational structure was functioning well, our information systems were developing nicely, and we had climbed out of the financial black hole. Then, suddenly, our ailing leader retired. In October of 1982, after twenty-nine years, the Bowen era was stunningly over.

The board appointed its chairman, A. Frank Smith, Jr., as interim president and announced the formation of a committee to conduct a national search for a new, permanent president. Frank Smith was Houston establishment. Of medium height, he had a commanding presence, yet he always seemed relaxed, comfortable. Above icy blue eyes, he had a full head of pure white hair. He always wore navy blue solid or pinstriped suits and soft black loafers. For years, I had admired his style of dress and carriage and I changed my wardrobe to mimic his.

Frank Smith's appointment was a crushing blow to me! While I realized that I was only 39 years old (and that might be a problem with some members of the board, whose average age was 61), I felt that my leadership performance as chief operating officer should have brought me the top job. The counsel from chairman Smith that my position as president, if I were selected, would be stronger because of the national search process, was of little comfort as the search began.

If the Medicare Prospective Payment Act hadn't been introduced in Congress, I might not have been chosen. The Methodist staff's analysis of the act indicated significant problems for teaching hospitals and large referral centers. A system that standardized payments to hospitals, regardless of the complexity of the patient's illness, would be devastating for our kind of institution. We had to get that law changed before it passed. I told chairman Smith that I was going to take a group of executives to Washington and attempt to change the law; he said he would come with me. Over the course of the next few weeks in the nation's capital two things happened. First, with the leadership of a truly great Texan, Senator Lloyd Bentsen, we amended the proposed law to give special consideration to national and international referral centers. Methodist was mentioned prominently in the Senator's introduction of the amendment. Second, Frank Smith and I grew to like and respect one another. That was the start of one of the most important and enjoyable relationships in my life.

In Houston, the board's search committee continued its work, interviewing several very prominent and well-known hospital executives and another inside candidate. Finally, it was my turn. I was last. I walked into the stately Fondren room and took the place indicated for me at the head of the table. Leading board members and physicians filled the chairs around what had been the dining room table of Mrs. Walter Fondren, the wife of a founder of Exxon. After a few minutes of light conversation, the committee chairman went right to the point: "Larry, if you were named president of the hospital, what would you do." That was a question I had spent my entire career preparing to answer. In the next fifteen minutes, I outlined my goals for Methodist: a strong strategic planning process; financial strength; a better relationship with Baylor College of Medicine; a motivated and informed workforce; patient service excellence; and top quality programs for patient care, teaching, and research. When I finished, a tougher question came: "If you are not named president, will you stay?" I had given that an inordinate amount of anguished thought. "I love The Methodist Hospital and I would hate to leave it, but I am capable of being an outstanding chief executive officer. If I'm not selected, I will leave." The interview was over; I walked back to my office. Within ten minutes Frank Smith came in to my office. "Larry, the search committee voted unanimously to name you president and chief executive officer of The Methodist Hospital."

"I accept."

The board acted on its search committee's recommendation at its meeting in July, 1983. At the conclusion of that meeting, Frank came into my office, congratulated me and said. "Now, my job's done. I'm going back downtown to the firm; call me if you need me." I said, "Look, chief, this has been a great partnership these last few months. I want you to stay involved. I'm creating an office for the chairman. Please, stay." He did.

With my promotion came promotions for my team. My senior vice presidents became my executive vice presidents and one of them, Ron Girotto, became both chief operating officer and chief financial officer. That decision later revealed itself to be a stroke of genius, as the usual war between operations and finance was taken from the battlefield of the chief executive's office and planted squarely on Ron's capable shoulders. For the move to be successful, I knew it would require outstanding performance. Ron never disappointed me.

We set an incredibly brisk management pace. After nine months of stalled uncertainty about Methodist's future leadership, the team was ready to run. In the early months, we structured the strategic planning process that we used so successfully for my entire tenure; we addressed service problems; and we created a new relationship with our employees.

Along the way, we reorganized our corporate structure. We created The Methodist Hospital System. We built a large and successful network of owned, managed and affiliated hospitals in Texas and Louisiana. Run superbly by executive vice president Mike Williamson, it grew to be the second largest not-for-profit, non-Catholic network in the country. We used the network to pursue growth in admissions among our foreign patients. We signed affiliation agreements with private hospitals in Mexico, Turkey, Greece, Guatemala, Italy, and Peru, as well as other countries. We took to these facilities delegations of physicians, who lectured, saw patients and, if appropriate, referred them to Methodist. Every year, more than 200 Methodist physicians admitted patients from more than 80 foreign countries. At one point, four percent of Methodist's patients were foreign, but they accounted for 20 percent of its net income.

Clinically, we made the decision to re-enter the transplant business. Heart transplant pioneer Dr. DeBakey came to see me and strongly recommended that we do so. Unfortunately, there were still serious misgivings among leaders of our medical staff about the transplants done in the late 1960s. I'm sure Dr. DeBakey would have liked me to act faster, but I took the time to employ a task force to study the issue. I included some of the leading transplant critics on it. Working through the issues with them wasn't easy, but the unanimous recommendation from the group was to resume transplantation. However, this time it would be in a formal organizational structure and address all types of human transplantation, not just hearts. Dr. DeBakey was named to head The Methodist Hospital/Baylor College of Medicine Multi-Organ Transplantation Center. Financially, we were beginning to do well. We had made a serious institutional commitment through our planning process to be financially secure in the future. We couldn't predict the future, but we knew that a strong financial war chest created strategic options. We had accumulated enough money—reserves of about $50,000,000—to require that we hire outside money managers. We had come to a new level. Then, crisis struck.

Following the Hermann Hospital scandal, a television investigative reporter did a story on "affluent" Methodist Hospital and its "inadequate" amount of charity care. Seizing the moment, Texas' opportunistic attorney general, Jim Mattox, began an "investigation" of our organization. Over the course of this skirmish, which ultimately ran on for eight years, we managed to build a new patient tower and a new, 25-story professional building, to increase admissions and outpatient services, and to improve the financial condition of the System. But through that period, the attorney general and his staff were a spectral presence. Ultimately, Methodist triumphed when a lawsuit filed by Mattox was thrown out of court in a summary judgment. But, as the old judicial saying goes, "you can beat the rap, but you can't beat the ride." It was one wild ride.

During that period, I was active in healthcare industry politics. My long-time friend, Horace Cardwell of Lufkin, Texas, a former chairman of the American Hospital Association and an industry politician of the first rank, took me on as a "project," running political campaigns for me at the state and national level. Horace was one of a kind. He was tall and brash and could be loud. He wore cowboy boots. At a cocktail party he would throw an arm around your shoulder, often forgetting that he held a drink in his hand. A wet back was a small price to pay for his friendship. I loved him. He politicked me onto the boards of the Texas Hospital Association, the American Hospital Association, and the American College of Healthcare Executives. He campaigned for me to be chairman of each and he won. He won. I didn't.

The pace of my life was frantic. I loved it. But, nature has a way of telling you to slow down. On a crisp March morning in1988, I woke at the usual 5 a.m., showered, dressed, and left for the office. After thirty minutes there, I got back in my car and started the three-mile drive to downtown Houston for a meeting. Halfway there, the pain started. It was like a belt wrapped around my chest and it was being pulled tighter and tighter. My left shoulder ached and, oddly, my left wrist hurt. I drove two more blocks before I turned back to the hospital. I knew almost immediately that I was having a heart attack. My car's speed increased as the pain did. Minutes seemed to last and last. I wasn't sure I would make it. Finally. I pulled into Methodist's emergency exit, got out of the car, and walked into the ER. Emily, one of our great emergency nurses was in the hallway as I entered. "Are you all right?" she asked.

"I think I'm having a heart attack."

"Come lie down, you do look a little peaked," she said.

My first question to Bill Winters, my friend and cardiologist, when he arrived at my gurney minutes later was: "I am eligible for tPa, aren't I?" The blood clot dissolving drug was then being tested in a national clinical trial. On my watch, Methodist had been one of only five centers in the country to participate in the trial. "Yes, you are," came Bill's answer. Quickly, I was diagnosed as having a myocardial infarction, whisked to the coronary care unit, and infused with tPa.

Within an hour of the onset of pain as I was driving to town, the clot dissolved. The following day, I had an angioplasty (the first of many to come in the ensuing years), which opened the stricture in the offending artery. Miraculously, there was no damage to the heart muscle. I had finessed a heart attack. Two days later, I walked boldly into a meeting of all of our system executives at an area hotel. I told them I wanted to welcome them to Houston; what I really wanted was for them to see that their CEO was not incapacitated. While there was little physical damage from the episode, there was the expected mental and emotional impact of a 44-year old, hard-charging executive confronting his own mortality—in my case, once again confronting his own mortality.

Through the years in the corner office, Betty and I were reaching the conclusion that we did not want to spend the rest of our lives together. She was, I believe, finally tired of being defined by her husband and her children. She wanted to be known as Betty Mathis, not Mrs. Larry Mathis, Julie's mother, or Jennifer's mother. Contemplating breaking up a twenty-five year partnership brought considerable emotional pain, but once we had worked through it, we created our own model for divorce. We set criteria: we agreed that we would be fair; we would remain friends; we would split everything equally; we would use one attorney, hers; and, we would tell both girls at the same time.

Over the course of five months, we sold our farm and liquidated our investments and accounts, sweeping the money into a new joint account, to be divided equally. Two weeks before the divorce was to be final, Julie and Jennifer came home from school. In an emotional meeting, we broke the news. But, two weeks later, we gathered at our favorite Chinese restaurant on the day the court papers were signed for a family dinner—with champagne. We toasted each of the girls for their school accomplishments. I toasted Betty and her new found freedom. She raised her glass and toasted me.

In 1993, our planning process provoked a mission conference. A mission conference is usually necessary when momentous change is occurring. That change was the growth of managed care in the Houston market and our physicians' perceived need to contract for it. Until that time, our successful strategy had been to be the high quality alternative to managed care. Over the course of several months, key stakeholders met and struggled with the issues. In May of 1994, the decision was made to change from being a system supporting a teaching hospital to a healthcare system configured for lower cost managed care. That decision had immediate implications. The management team that had brought us to this point would have to undo much of its work. The programs we were invested in and had created would have to change, sometimes painfully.

We realized that our costs were high for the managed care environment. Over the course of 15 months, we reduced the workforce from 7,025 to 4,900. With other reductions, we took $125 million out of our expense budget. Over twelve months, we went from no managed care contracts to thirty-one and moved the city's largest HMO's business to Methodist from Hermann Hospital. We created a primary care physician group, acquired Houston's largest visiting nurse association, and began building community health centers. We created Methodist Care, our own health maintenance organization. That much change, that fast, is very hard on an organization. (See the Sumo maxim).

Change in the organization was tough for me, but a change in my personal life offset its difficulty. After four years as a divorced man, in 1995 I was married to Diane Peterson. A Pennsylvania native, Diane had formed her own consulting firm in Houston after a distinguished executive career in Pittsburgh and Houston hospitals. I had known her professionally for years through the American College of Healthcare Executives. She is a remarkable woman. She is beautiful on the outside, but even more beautiful on the inside. She brought style and grace to my bachelor home and made it a serene place for two. She is intelligent and accomplished. She is my wife, my colleague, my lover, and my best friend. She is also my hobby.

In October of 1997, I stood at the podium in the ballroom of the stately River Oaks Country Club. Before me were hundreds of people—board members, physicians, executives, and volunteers—gathered to wish me well in my retirement as CEO. It was my turn to speak, to thank them for the board's generous resolution and for the nice words of praise. As I looked at the faces that I had known so well for 27 years, a lump formed in my throat. It had all gone so fast!

I smiled. I began to speak, to reminisce about my long career at TMH. I told them about the day legendary Texas oilman Perry Bass came into the executive offices and asked to speak to Ted Bowen, then the administrator. I stepped out of my office, introduced myself as Mr. Bowen's assistant, and asked if I could help him. He smiled the sweetest smile at me and taught me one of his own maxims: "I never deal with a one-feathered Indian." I told them about the day a very unusual woman came into the offices. She was wearing what looked to me like a tennis outfit—short white skirt, matching blouse—but, she had on purple tights under the skirt and had a large yellow scarf draped around her shoulders. She had a red bow in her grayish, yellow hair. She acted strangely. She asked to speak to Mr. Bowen. I told her I was Mr. Bowen's assistant. He wasn't available, could I help? Well, she said she had met with Mr. Bowen twenty years ago to present an idea she had: combine all the dietary facilities in the Texas Medical Center and serve all the hospitals from that one facility. I asked her what Mr. Bowen had told her back then. She said he told her that her idea was twenty years ahead of its time. I looked at her, and said. "I think it is still twenty years ahead of its time." She left. I told them about the time Tony's restaurant told me to wear a tie, about the time I canoed through the streets of Houston to the hospital. I thanked them for the wonderful blessing and opportunity they had given me to be a part of that great institution for my entire career and their leader for the last fourteen years. And, then, in closing, I told them that it seemed just yesterday that I stood across the street from Methodist, a candidate for a residency, and had my epiphany.

In The Organization

The object is to win!

I stood on the corner of Fannin and Dryden and looked across the street at the hospital with the distinctive mosaic mural across its front. I had come to interview for a hospital administrative residency at The Methodist Hospital of Houston in the world famous Texas Medical Center. My college days were over. My five years as an infantry officer were history. As I stood staring, in my only civilian suit, I had my epiphany.

It was an incredible, immediate knowing. And, a certainty. I was staring at my professional destiny. In a sudden rush, I understood that I was not here, at this place in time, to try for a one-year educational experience—the residency; I was going to run this hospital one day.

As I look back now on that moment, I am tempted to explain it as youthful arrogance (I was 28 at the time) or supreme overconfidence (I had just survived a war) or perhaps something else within me. It certainly would have been arrogant of me to assume that I would someday be the Chief Executive Officer of the practice home of Dr. Michael DeBakey, the site of many of the early heart transplants, the hospital of choice of the Duke of Windsor, the battleground of the uncivil war between legendary heart surgeons Cooley and DeBakey. But, it wasn't from within me. Wherever that message came from, it was clear, distinct, over-powering and completely outside of and apart from Larry Mathis. Along with that message of predestination came realization: *It will take everything I've got to make that happen.*

I squared my shoulders, and somewhat shaken, crossed Fannin Street to begin what became my career-long quest. I entered The Methodist Hospital that day focused on winning. "The object is to win," I told myself. I defined ultimate winning as becoming the CEO. But, a lot of interim winning was going to be required to reach that destination. Winning respect, winning choice assignments, winning followers, promotions, skirmishes, friendships, and battles. That much winning was going to take commitment. It was going to take focus.

I made the decision to make my new career priority-one in my life. For the next 12 years on my journey to the corner office, I subordinated everything to this goal. If a school play starring my daughter conflicted with a business engagement, my daughter didn't have a father in the audience. The first year of my career, I was in the office every one of the 365 days. That's right, all weekdays, every Saturday, every Sunday, every holiday. That focus on winning was successful; it did result in a steady rise through the executive ranks and, twelve years later, into the CEO position. However...

However, through that period of incredible focus and commitment, I did lose a few things and learn a few things. My marriage didn't survive the journey and I lost a lot of time with my two wonderful daughters. Time and times that cannot be regained. There was no room for other interests and for other pursuits. There were no hobbies. No golf. Along the way there were the stress-related ailments: high blood pressure and heart disease. I may not have been a balanced person; but, I certainly was focused.

What have I learned? First, be careful how you define winning in a career and in a life. I don't regret my focus on winning the CEO job at one specific institution; however, today I do have a more realistic view of the costs involved. If I had fully understood the costs at the head of the trail, I might have thought more carefully before starting down it. Defining winning in only one dimension—career, as I did—was probably wrong. Giving definition to success in several facets of life is probably better—and carries less risk of failure.

Which brings me to the second thing I learned. If the object is to win, and you are totally focused and committed to such a goal, what happens if you don't win? Devastation, personal and professional, can be the result of failure to accomplish an overpowering single objective. If you decide to seek the grail, you must be prepared for the possibility of failure. What will be the impact on your life, career, relationships, and self-esteem if you are found wanting? Or, if the grail simply cannot be found?

In my view, most successful chief executive officers are winners. They are the individuals who have proven themselves (usually through years of hard work, sacrifice, and solid achievement; not to mention political acumen). But, CEOs are not the only winners. If you have the fire in the belly (as I did) to hold the top job, my advice is to go for it. Be mindful of the price you will pay, but go for it. If the fire is not there, define winning in another way.

The subjugation of women throughout history is mankind's loss.

It was quite an honor for a healthcare CEO and an ex-infantryman to be invited by the U.S. Navy to fly out to one of our nuclear-powered aircraft carriers to watch flight operations. I was one of a group of civilian VIPs, invited for public relations purposes, who climbed out of the plane onto the deck of the USS Abraham Lincoln. For 24 hours, we observed carrier operations and watched—both during daylight and, terrifyingly, in the black Pacific night—young pilots make their first qualifying landings on the deck of an aircraft carrier. We went throughout the ship, learning and marveling. For an old infantry "ground-pounder" like, me it was awesome to contemplate the sheer power of this largest and most sophisticated machine of war. I was incredulous to learn that the average age of the crew, officers included, was only nineteen. And nearly half were women!

Coming to comprehend the intellect, creativity, innovation, and leadership potential of the female half of the population has been the result of a long and difficult journey for me. Growing up in Kansas in the 1940s, 50s, and 60s was the equivalent of earning a master's in macho and a PhD in paternalism. Dads were the breadwinners; Moms kept house. Their little boys could aspire to be doctors, lawyers, firemen, engineers, and carpenters. Their little girls were expected to be housewives. If a girl were unlucky enough to be unwed, then she could consider the acceptable female occupations: secretary, nurse, or teacher.

Men were men: that is, strong, uncomplaining, hard working, hard drinking, and ready to fight at the drop of a hat. Women were women: that is, beautiful, compliant, loving, pregnant (preferably with males) and ready to whip up a casserole at a moment's notice. I bought it all. And, to make matters worse, my first profession was the ultimate macho choice—The United States Army Infantry.

Combat is man's work! The leadership skills I learned in the army were masculine, transferred almost whole from the sports fields to the killing fields. You didn't see many feminine attributes among those parachuting from C130 aircraft or dodging AK47 rounds in the rice paddies. Men fought. Men died. Men ruled. What was wrong with that?

On my personal journey of growth and discovery, I have come to see that as an outrage and a tragedy.

My journey had learning stops in marriage, in divorce, in the experience of helping two delightful daughters grow into accomplished young women, and in remarriage. From those personal relationships, I knew that women had just as much intelligence, charisma, drive—any desirable trait I could name—as men. Then I came to spend my career in an organization of women—the hospital. At Methodist, about 80% of the employees were female. During 27 years, I worked with truly outstanding women professionals, managers, and executives. I was educated, enlightened, and changed by them.

Women now make up about half of the students in law and medical schools. In healthcare administration, it is over 60 percent.

While the women of my generation, those who grew up during the 1940s and 1950s, will probably not come to full power, the new generation of women who fill the ranks of the medical, law, business, and healthcare administration schools today will bring into being a new majority in those professions and with it, will change the balance of power. As they rise in organizations, they will create a new environment at the top, one that is a comfortable fit for the female leader, thus overcoming the current single largest barrier to success: lack of "fit" with the other members of the top leadership team— males.

Organizations are places of chaos.

"A man just fell off the Fondren building!" The shout from the emergency room nurse sent an electric shock through my body. I ran after her, heading toward I didn't know what. We raced down the first floor wheelchair ramp and out onto the hot parking lot. Side by side we ran to the Fondren building construction fence. Inside the gate, we saw him. He had fallen from nine stories above, landing doubled over with his legs stretched out under his torso. The impact had split him open and his spine was exposed. With tears in her eyes, the nurse vainly applied the stethoscope. He was dead. We later learned that he was the boss of the bricklaying crew who was working on the exterior of a new addition to the building. The crane operator had delivered a pallet of bricks to the work site. The boss had given the crane operator the all-clear signal to move the hook, but it accidentally became entangled in the scaffold; as the operator pulled the hook away, the scaffold came with it. Two crewmen grabbed steel supports and held on, but the boss was tossed overboard. Accident.

Late one night, at a remote facility we called the Annex, a man slipped in a side door, went on to a patient care unit and sexually assaulted one of our patients. Rape.

An enraged psychiatry patient somehow got hold of a butcher knife and rampaged through the psych ward, killing one and wounding two others. Murder.

A respected surgeon regularly hit the bottle in the mornings. Alcoholism.

71

A bright, up-and-coming young physician struggled to find ways to keep his Percodan habit supplied, while a distinguished older physician administered a patient's Demerol shot into his own thigh. Drug abuse.

One-third to one-half of the hospital's linen inventory disappeared annually; an executive padded his expense account. Theft.

Late one night, a despondent student from nearby Rice University, climbed to the top of one of our professional office building garages and leapt ten floors to his death. Suicide.

These are only a few examples of the chaotic things I have seen during my career in hospitals. And, I have barely touched on examples of less deadly chaos in the executive suite.

Organizations are places of chaos because they are people places. Along with their good qualities, people in organizations are liars, cheats, and thieves; they are drug addicts, alcoholics, and criminals; they covet, they envy, and they connive. In short, people in organizations have the same frailties and shortcomings as people everywhere.

Executives, or at least the good ones, crave bringing order out of the human, organizational chaos. They work, they sweat, they lead, they motivate, they inspire, and they succeed. Maybe they succeed often—consistently. And then they fail...becoming part of the chaos. They become petty, vindictive, protective, paranoid, and, Valium sleepers. Therefore...there is no therefore—as in most corporations.

This maxim is, obviously, very negative. I, on the other hand, tended to be a positive and optimistic executive. Today, it is hard for me to believe that I ever sank that low and wrote something like that. But, I did.

Here's why. My only organizational experience before joining Methodist was the military. There I spent five years learning the science of war and one of those years, in Vietnam, learning the chaos of war. I left the Army seeking a nobler, a finer, a more idealistic way to spend the rest of my life. In graduate school, I convinced myself that a career in a hospital would meet that need; that a hospital would be nobler, finer—the ideal. And, in many ways, it was. But, through the years, accidents, rapes, murders, alcoholism, drug abuse, theft, and suicide, combined with the competitive combat in the executive ranks, enlightened me. Even hospitals, havens of healing and caring, are places of chaos. Places of chaos, precisely because they are people places.

At its peak as an employer, Methodist had a payroll of more than 7,000. That was larger than the population of many of the small towns I had lived in as I grew up. That many people in one place brought with them all varieties of human condition and behavior. As idealistic as I was, I realized that a chief executive had no more ability to control the actions and behaviors of that many people than did a mayor of a small town in Oklahoma or Iowa.

Both within my organization and within the industry, I had also seen the results of chaos in the executive suite. Excellent colleagues, ones with sterling track records and signal accomplishments, had been burned out, passed over, tripped up, sloshed, and addicted. Events beyond their control ruined their careers and sometimes their lives. Just as often, and even worse, events *within* their control did the same.

I wrote this maxim when I was at an extremely low point in my career, when I was a number two man, without much hope of becoming a number one. For me, the lesson was two-fold. First, even the most optimistic and upbeat executive can get discouraged when organizational chaos reigns or the executive suite wars become unbearable. But, second, no matter how bad it seems, you can pick yourself up, dust yourself off, and get back on for the ride. Somehow, out of that dark time, I was able to get to the number one job.

If you find yourself in one of these deep valleys, remind yourself that the experience can temper and strengthen you for the days ahead, make you wiser and more compassionate, and make the coming view from the peak that much more stunning.

The executive's joy in being "right" diminishes
if it results in unemployment.

Most executives have strong egos. They are, by and large, a self-confident group. They have done well enough in college to qualify for a spot in graduate school; they have earned their advanced degrees and worked themselves into the executive ranks. Most are intelligent, are hardworking, and have a history of success. A trait they have in common: They enjoy being right.

They enjoy being right about their organizations' tactics, strategies, procedures, and policies. They like to be right in the eyes of their bosses and they want their subordinates to believe that they are right about all the important things. They have strong opinions about what should be done and how it should be done. Unfortunately, in organizations, things often are done differently. To the executive, "differently" means wrong, if it doesn't agree with his preconceived "right" way of doing things.

How do you handle an organizational decision that you just know is wrong, particularly when *you* have the right answer? Interestingly, there are two ways: the right way and the wrong way. First, the wrong way. As an executive, you know that the new personnel policy is just pig-headedly bad and that it will have an adverse effect on both hiring and retention of key employees. But the CEO is leaning toward approving it. You tell the CEO it is a mistake and give him your recommendation for how to proceed. He approves the

75

pig-headed policy anyway. Then you tell your colleagues, your subordinates, your employees, and anyone else who will listen that the policy is a bad one and you predict it will fail. You do nothing to help implement it; you undercut it and criticize it at every turn. When, sure enough, it does fail, you remind your colleagues that you told them so. Not only will such behavior make you unpopular in the organization, it could hurt your chances for advancement. It might even get you squeezed out.

The right way? First, *do* give your opinion to the CEO (only if you report directly to him) or to your boss. Carefully explain what you believe the problems are with the policy and give your recommendations for a solution. When a poor decision is made, keep quiet. It may very well be terrible, but, once made, it *is* the decision. Try to help make it work. If it fails, keep your opinions about it to yourself.

Throughout an executive career, you will see many decisions with which you do not agree. If you see them as a junior executive, keep in mind that those above you who make those decisions may have more information than you have access to, or that it may be tactically wrong but strategically right—a sacrificed pawn to capture a knight. If you are on the senior management team, you have a responsibility to give your very best judgments and recommendations, then to support the decision that is made, wrong or not. That is expected of a team player. If you insist on crowing about "right," you may find the joy diminished if you are in the unemployment line.

Like all generalizations, there is an exception. Of course, be a team player and support even bad operations decisions. However, it is entirely different if you know the decision to be either unethical or illegal. You must in either case do everything in your power to change the decision to a proper one. If, nonetheless, the wrong decision is taken, then there is the joy of being right, even in the unemployment line. The unemployment line is better than a ruined reputation. It is *far* better than the penitentiary.

In a personality conflict with the boss,
the subordinate is always at fault.

In the executive suite, I knew of very few personality conflicts between a subordinate and his boss that were resolved in favor of the subordinate. While it may not be literally true that the subordinate is *always* the one at fault, it is in all practicality true. He may be wrong, but he is still the boss. It is highly unlikely that he will alter his behavior or change his personality to fit better with one of his subordinates. The lesson then, for the aspiring young executive, is: "Get along with your boss."

In an executive career, you will likely encounter a significant number of bosses. It is equally likely that their personalities and styles will cover the leadership spectrum, from charming, inspirational leader to stupid and stubborn ogre. Having an inspirational boss is manna from heaven; every day is a blessing. Having one who is incompetent or abusive is a lead weight on the spirit. You have to learn to get along with both. If you have drawn a bad boss, find a way out—new job, reassignment, or promotion. But until you are rid of him, *adapt* your personality to his. If you are the subordinate, you have already lost a personality conflict with your boss. It wasn't a fair fight.

People do not all think in the same terms.

It took me a long time to figure this one out. As a young executive trying to be an inclusive and participatory leader, I would lay out proposals for my team of department managers. They were logical because I have a logical mind; that's the way my mental processes work. I was often stunned by the comments and reactions I got to some of the proposed actions. If we were discussing a simple change in personnel policy, for example, we might not reach consensus at all. I would show how logical the change was, while a team member might object emotionally to the policy. Another might chime in that change was bad because it would cost us money out of our own pockets. Over time, I concluded that each team member processed information and made decisions in individualistic and personal ways. To be a successful participatory leader, I realized, I needed to figure out how each of my colleagues thought.

I was amazed to discover how different they were. Team members could come to strongly held, yet widely divergent, "moral and ethical" conclusions on the same question depending upon how they thought. One manager was process oriented; *how* the decision got made was the critical element. Another had a financial orientation; if the numbers worked, then the decision was correct. One was relationship orientated; each decision was judged by its impact on individuals and groups. Still another had a personal orientation; he evaluated decisions according to their benefit or detriment to him.

Learning that people process information in different ways is just the beginning for an executive. By assessing each team member's orientation, you will have a good idea of how each of your associates will react to a given proposal, issue, or decision. Then you can frame debate and discussion in ways that speak to each team member's mental processes.

Obviously, this maxim is not limited to your organizational subordinates. It should shape your relationship with your boss as well. Understanding that you and your boss process information and decisions differently can be a powerful insight, so it is incumbent on you to know how the boss thinks if your relationship is going to be successful.

By the same token, figuring out how influential physicians' thought processes work can also be illuminating. Unfortunately, in my experience, when it comes to physicians participating in organizational decisions, personal orientation predominates—"How will this decision affect me and my practice?" But, knowing they think that way means that you can deal with those personal concerns in the process of handling various issues. Your leadership effectiveness will be enhanced if you analyze how your organization's key stakeholders think, then use that insight to interact more persuasively with them.

Nothing is confidential.

When I began my executive career at Methodist, I was surprised to see that almost every memo was marked "Personal and Confidential." Coming from service as an officer in the army, I was used to classified documents. "Secret" and "Top Secret" were terms that meant something serious—clear expectations that the documents would be handled carefully and would not be disclosed to unauthorized personnel. I assumed that "Personal and Confidential" meant something similar in the civilian world. But, I was wrong. From the very beginning, it was clear that the contents of such memos were widely known and discussed—perhaps furtively, though, since it meant breaking the rules. Over time, I learned that in organizations (and maybe particularly hospital organizations), nothing is confidential.

Confidential information represents power. Those who are privy to it, have power over those who don't. But power is worthless, unless it is used. Therefore, the first rule of confidential information is that it is immediately, selectively shared. Executives share it with their allies and supporters to demonstrate their power. Secrets are immediately transmitted through the power networks in organizations.

Everyone has a confidential friend with whom we share everything—including secrets. As soon as something is branded "confidential," it is flagged in our minds as something to be shared with that person. Sometimes the special friend is a spouse or significant other, sometimes not. When it is not, the network for disseminating confidential information is that much larger. Within 24 hours of the publication of a confidential memo, those who received it have selectively shared it with organizational allies, friends, and spouses; each of those has potentially shared it as well. And so it spreads like a virus.

Labeling a memo "Confidential" calls attention to its subject matter and removes the necessity of judgment by the receiver as to its importance. If it's marked confidential, the information must be important enough to be shared among the intimate circle. I often thought that a truly private memo would be better handled with no indicator of sensitivity, since some of the recipients might judge the news to be inconsequential and, therefore, not share it.

Having made those observations, I developed a bias against "Confidential" communications of any sort. As CEO, I asked our team not to send "Personal and Confidential" memoranda. Our standard was that anything we wrote, should be written as if it might appear on the front page of the *Houston Chronicle*. It was amazing how our writing styles changed.

There is no perfect organizational structure.

As a young executive at Methodist, I watched several reorganizations of the hospital's departments. The president would use three-by-five inch cards with a department's name on each. He would group the cards together, then write an executive's name on top. In some of those shufflings, vice presidents wound up with a strange assortment of unrelated departments and functions; e.g., dietary, legal affairs, orthopedics, pharmacy. I told myself that one day I would do it better. I knew there was a perfect organizational structure for a hospital and I was going to find it. After long experience with organizing and reorganizing healthcare departments, divisions, and corporations, I now know better.

When I became CEO, I organized along functional lines: patient services, financial services, staff services, and support services, with each division containing related departments and functions. I assigned executives to each. I *knew* I had it right. As a plan of organization, it worked about as well as any I ever tried, but there were problems with communications and cooperation across divisional lines.

Over time, I realized that an organizational structure is not an organizational solution. It is a temporary alignment of work and responsibility to address specific needs. Organizing for increased financial control is different than organizing to encourage more entrepreneurial thinking; structuring for faster decision-making is different than structuring for executive development. I learned that while each reorganization offered strengths and advantages, it also brought corresponding weaknesses and disadvantages.

What finally worked best for me was a double organizational structure. The basic configuration for administration, personnel, and reporting was the functional structure. It was permanent. The second element was the task force structure. It pulled together the necessary people from the various functional divisions to address specific organizational needs or challenges such as building a new facility, assessing an acquisition, or fighting an assault by the Attorney General. Each had a multidivisional task force. The combination structure worked well.

When you reorganize, whether it is your department, your division, your corporation, or your healthcare system, think through specifically what it is you want to accomplish. Know that while the new configuration may meet your goals, it will create other problems. And, know that it will not be perfect; it will not be final.

On executive recruitment from the outside:
You don't get better people—just different people.

Why is it that so many hospital and system boards tend to favor recruitment from outside of the organization to fill key executive vacancies? Why is it, too, that after an appropriate honeymoon, the imported executive often disappoints those who recruited him?

The unknown executive always looks so much better than the fellow down the hall. That is understandable. The internal candidate for the CEO job is a known quantity. If he has been in the organization for any length of time at all, his strengths and his weaknesses are both evident. The insider has had the opportunity to display them in many settings and to a variety of groups. Physicians have seen the effect of his decisions; employees have witnessed a range of reactions and behaviors; board members have formed opinions of his capabilities and limitations. The insider is seen realistically— warts and all. Outsiders, on the other hand, enter the interview process at their very best. They have brief periods of exposure to key decision-makers. In those interactions, their only job is to highlight their strengths and conceal their weaknesses. Most of us can do that and do it well. Be confident. Be strong. Be wise. Be charming. It's work, but it is usually limited to a few hours. Unfortunately, it's not a realistic view.

Once chosen, the outsider walks onto the organization's stage. He (or she) strides into full view. The range of his personality and behaviors is on display. Because all executives have pluses and minuses, it is soon apparent that the organization has not recruited a better executive than the insider—just a different one.

I decided early to favor the insider. When I was promoted to senior vice president of Methodist in 1978 the president assigned several vice presidents to work with me in my new division. For nearly twenty years, three of those colleagues stayed with me as my management team. I hadn't picked them to work for me, someone else had. When I was promoted to executive vice president and COO in 1980, they became my senior vice presidents and division heads. When I was named CEO in 1983, they became my executive vice presidents and later, in subsequent system reorganizations, became presidents of subsidiaries I chaired.

The stability of that senior management team created a steady work environment. There was no revolving door of failed senior executives. Employees, physicians, volunteers, vendors, and community leaders knew that the team was in place and was going to be in place for the long term. I think that my bias to "play the hand I was dealt" created a team that signaled security and confidence to the rest the organization and to those outside as well.

I'm not recommending that outside recruitment never be used. There are many reasons why new blood might be needed: to obtain skills lacking in the organization; to introduce a different perspective. But absent compelling reasons, I believe it should be viewed as an organizational and a leadership failure if a strong and capable inside candidate is not groomed and ready to step into a key position.

The true leadership task is to organize and lead to success a team of other human beings, without much regard to the team's composition. If success doesn't come, it's a failure of leadership—not a team failure.

Bum Phillips, the down-to-earth, good-ole-boy who coached the Houston Oilers in the 1980s, probably said it best. He was talking about what it takes to be a great football coach. He named one of the very best—Don Shula, coach of the indomitable Miami Dolphins. Bum said of Shula, "he can take his'n and beat your'n or he can take your'n and beat his'n." For a leader, that about says it all.

Leadership

There is dignity and worth in every person.

During my life, my jobs have included janitor, soda jerk, stock boy, printer, newspaper reporter, bellhop, truck driver, platoon leader, battalion advisor, college professor, administrative resident, junior executive, senior executive, chief executive officer and consultant. Through all of them, except for differences in age, I was pretty much the same person—same personality, same sense of self, same values. But, I have not always been treated like the same person; sometimes people defined me by the job I held and treated me accordingly—sometimes well, sometimes not. I knew that I was just as good a person when I was driving a truck as I was when I was teaching a college class; I had the same sense of self worth when I swept floors as when I wrote a story for the newspaper. I tried to do every job to the very best of my ability.

Perhaps because of some of these experiences, as a chief executive officer, I was constantly aware of the dignity and worth that each stakeholder in our organization brought to it. I tried to treat everyone—surgeon, laundress, board member, gardener, nurse—the same: with fairness, openness, and respect. I have known executives who are superb at relating to their organizational superiors, but denigrate their subordinates. They schmooze their bosses; they scream at their secretaries. Such behavior represents a failure of leadership values. You can't effectively lead others if you do not respect the dignity and worth of every person in the organization. Respect is the very foundation of leadership.

The troops eat first.

When the U.S. army infantry is in the field, its officers make sure that the soldiers receive their meals before the officers eat. It is a small thing, but it says big things about leadership. It says that the soldiers, "the troops" in army jargon, are the most important part of an organization that is made up of soldiers, non-commissioned officers, and commissioned officers. It says that the highest-ranking officers have a duty to take care of the troops and to put them ahead of the officers' own welfare. This is a uniquely American and democratic view of military leadership, one not found in many armies around the world, in most of which the officers set themselves apart as aristocracy. The concept of putting the troops first may have something to do with the fact that the United States won two world wars and has emerged as the only super power at the dawn of a new millennium.

This is a lesson in leadership that I learned while I served in the army and it has served me well as a healthcare executive. When I began my career as a leader at Methodist, I was amazed at the work of the caregivers. They not only gave their time to the organization for pay, they gave their lives to the care of their patients. I soon came to believe that, not only were they the hands of the organization, they were its heart. I put them first.

A leader should stand in awe of front line employees who are exceptional at what they do. It might be a rifleman taking a bunker. It might be a salesman closing a sale. It might be a nurse comforting a dying man. And, in the case of the caregiver, awe is the appropriate word. A hospital is not a building with a cross on it. It is the many kind faces and caring hands of those who treat the sick and injured. Done well, lives are saved; physical, mental, and emotional scars are healed. Great care and service result.

A leader should have reverence for the tasks performed and the results achieved by such people. He should respect and admire them. He should put them first. And, that attitude will improve his judgments, shape his policies, and make him a better leader.

Leaders are more sensitive to the needs of their followers when their followers have guns.

I wrote this maxim as a part of my speech as the incoming chairman of the American College of Healthcare Executives, my professional society. I knew that the many military officers in the audience, those exceptional professionals who organize the delivery of military medicine around the world, would enjoy it. I wrote it to be humorous. In the context of a speech in a crowded ballroom in a Chicago hotel, it was. In another context, it wasn't funny at all.

Bam! That was a rifle shot. And, very close by. I had been standing near the bank of radios in the tactical operations control center at division headquarters in Lam Son, Republic of South Vietnam. I was getting ready to radio the battalions with daily instructions when I heard it. It had the unmistakable sound of one of the carbines with which the United States had armed the South Vietnamese soldiers. I ducked out of the bunker and crossed the path to the row of shacks that housed the division staff functions. A crowd had gathered at the second shack, surrounding a small Vietnamese private. His carbine lay on the ground. Inside, sitting in a chair behind one of the desks was his sergeant. He was dead—shot through the heart.

Later, we learned that the private was upset—and he believed, dishonored—by the way his sergeant treated him. So, he killed him. While not common, the history of warfare has many episodes of leaders killed by their own men. Late in the Vietnam War, there were news reports of officers being "fragged" by their troops. "Fragged" was slang for the practice of lobbing a fragmentation grenade into the sleeping quarters of officers—while they slept there.

Most of the U.S. infantry officers I knew were intelligent and sensitive to the difficulties of men in war. Officers often had to make awful decisions. They had to choose which individuals and which units would have the most dangerous assignments. When they told someone to take the point—the lead position—in a patrol, they were potentially conferring a death sentence. When they told someone to crawl into an enemy tunnel.... If things went wrong, and the men perceived it was the officer's fault, or if they believed he was incompetent, they might begin to think of ways to be rid of him. The officers I knew wanted to be sure that they were fair in spreading the risks of combat, playing no favorites. They paid exquisite attention to such things. And, they did everything tactically possible to minimize the dangers to their men.

Leadership in the executive suite is not combat leadership. But, I have often thought that some executives' leadership styles could have been improved if their followers had guns. I would be delighted to live in a world where no one ever again had to lead armed men into combat; but, I know that I am a better leader today because I did. I am pleased that the majority of my executive colleagues in the healthcare industry have not had to do so, but I suggest that every so often you ask yourselves: "What would I do now, if my people had guns?"

When you are out in front, you get shot at.

This is a lesson I learned as a young infantry officer in Vietnam; and one I relearned in a very different context as CEO of a prominent teaching hospital.

The infantry is the Queen of Battle. Its mission is to close with and destroy the enemy. That mission is the essence of war. The men whose job it is to "close with the enemy" know that they will be shot at. The first unit in the attack will be shot at first. The point man—the man out in front—is *sure* to get shot at. Being out in front in battle attracts fire. I know. I learned in combat.

Being out in front as an executive can also attract fire. Being an executive in a hospital or healthcare system is, by definition, being out in front. Hospitals are organizations where life and death dramas play out daily, where community health issues are confronted, where regulators inspect, where medical and business ethical issues swirl, where unions organize, where huge sums of cash flow. Hospitals are at the intersection of law, policy, and politics at the local, state, and federal levels. They are where many of society's unresolved issues wash up. Violence. Abuse. Guns. Drugs. In many cases, they are among their communities' largest employers. They are constant targets of litigation, regulation, and legislation. And, I repeat, they are places where huge sums of cash flow.

All of that makes America's hospitals very large, out-in-front targets and those of us who lead them are the organizational equivalent of infantry point men. We know, or should know, that we are going to get shot at. The shots can come from unions, regulators, litigators, legislators, competitors, and they can even come from our own troops— friendly fire: employees, physicians, volunteers, board members.

When I became CEO of Methodist, it was an internationally prominent teaching hospital. It was one of the nation's largest and it had a high political and media profile. I knew it was "out in front" and would be a constant target–from all the usual suspects as well as from enemies unseen and unnamed. Our management team resolved that we would conduct ourselves accordingly. We would manage so that we were constantly ready to be inspected, tested, singled-out, made an example of, sued, and challenged. We would use the highest ethics, make decisions based upon what was right, and make our business strategy public. If we found wrongdoing or criminality in our organization, we would address it, report it, and punish it. We would be zealous guardians of the organization's assets.

Thank God, we took that path! Throughout my years in the corner office of Methodist, the shots came. As part of the Attorney General's lawsuit over charity care, we were subjected to a coordinated barrage of regulatory, political, and media attacks. We endured constant state Department of Health inspections, a 48-month IRS audit, an attack video produced by the AG's office, a Sam Donaldson piece on *Prime Time*, a Dingell Committee hearing in Congress, and the constant attention of investigative reporters. All of that for eight years. [A play-by-play timetable is contained in the Government Section.] Not one single instance of wrongdoing or impropriety was turned up. Again, thank God, we decided to do it "right."

In America today, all hospitals are "out in front" in their communities. The executives who lead them are the point men and women for their organizations. If you are one of them, know that the shots will come. It is best to have your organization grounded in ethics and your team ready before the shooting starts.

Practice leadership in every setting. Not just at work.

When we moved to Houston for my administrative residency at Methodist, my family and I joined St. Luke's United Methodist Church. We chose to become United Methodists because it seemed to be an excellent middle ground between my Southern Baptist roots and my wife's Presbyterian upbringing. It didn't hurt that I had read The Methodist Hospital's bylaws, which stated the hospital administrator would "preferably be a Methodist." We chose St. Luke's specifically because it was the congregation of the hospital's administrator, many prominent board members, and leaders of the medical staff. In later years, I was fond of saying that I was a Southern Baptist before I became an Opportunist.

As I rose through the executive ranks at Methodist, I also was active in the leadership of the church. I joined its administrative board and served as a member for several years. I chaired the annual fund drive. And, at about the time I became the hospital's chief operating officer, I was elevated to chairman of the church's board. As a young member of the hospital's senior management, I had limited opportunity to demonstrate my leadership abilities to its board members. But, those individuals who were also members of St. Luke's church saw me perform as a leader and decision maker in a different setting. I believe that my performance as a church leader gave those board members who ultimately chose me as the hospital chief executive a view of my leadership capabilities that they never would have had of me as the number-two executive in the hospital organization. I worked in the lay leadership of the church because I believed in the church, its mission, and its beliefs. But, that work also showcased my leadership and helped to advance my career.

Showcasing your talents to those who can advance your career is just one reason to develop and demonstrate your leadership outside of your work environment. Another is practice. Successful leadership is like playing a violin; to be good at it you must practice. Leading in varied settings is good practice. Scout troop leader. PTA committee chairman. Sunday school class leader. Rotary Club president. Chairman of the Chamber of Commerce board. All of those jobs are leadership schools. All of them will help you be a better leader in the executive suite.

Another reason is representation. If you are a leader in an organization as important to the community as a hospital, you are expected to represent that enterprise to its community. One way you can do that is through leadership of civic activities. I always encouraged Methodist's managers and executives to be active leaders in their neighborhoods, their children's schools, their communities, and in their professional societies. I knew they were great leaders and I wanted to see those Methodist-brand stars in high profile positions, because I knew it would reflect positively on our entire organization.

Finally, there is one more reason to lead outside of the workplace: If you have the capability to lead, you have the responsibility to do so—in the executive suite, of course, but also wherever leadership is needed. Leading is what leaders do.

You don't get anywhere working for yourself—you must work for something bigger than yourself.

I've often thanked my guiding lights that my leadership talents found their home in healthcare. Hospitals transcend the world of everyday work because caring for and healing human beings is intrinsically noble; those who work there are blessed with a life-giving mission. Hospitals have the power to transform the caregiver and the leader of caregivers.

I used to wonder how the insurance broker, the automobile maker, or the shoe salesman found higher purpose in their worlds of work. Selling shoes isn't intrinsically noble, is it? But, I know there are men and women who sell shoes who find happiness and fulfillment in their work and in their lives. I stopped wondering about them when I recalled my father's work. George Mathis was a salesman. At various times, he worked for the Curtis Candy Company, the Singer Sewing Machine Company, and Standard Brands, Inc., the food distributor. I remember how Dad bought into those companies and believed in their products. He extolled the virtues of Lifesavers and other candies when he signed on with Curtis; when he joined Singer he truly believed that every American woman urgently needed a Singer sewing machine and, once she had one, she'd need a buttonholer and an embroidery attachment, too. More bobbins? As he ended his career with Standard Brands, he swore to anyone who would listen that Royal gelatin was the best there was. Growing up, whenever I referred to our dessert as "Jell-O," he corrected me: "It's Royal *gelatin*," he would say, "And, it's the best." He was an award-winning salesman, setting sales records and garnering honors in each of those companies.

In any industry, there are just jobs. Growing up, I had plenty of them—from soda jerk to truck driver. I had to spend my time and effort at these jobs to earn money. But, if I had to spend my entire life with that kind of relationship with work, my spirit would die. Health care is unique in that "just jobs" contribute to the noble cause. The hospital housekeeper isn't just sweeping a floor, but maintaining the environment for patient care. Working just for money is a prison. Working only to advance yourself is a lonely pursuit and an unworthy one.

As a healthcare executive, you are blessed with important and interesting work and you have a head start on taking your world of work to a higher plane of gratification and fulfillment. But whatever your position, to be truly successful you must find that higher plane. If you fill an executive position just for the money, sooner or later you will be exposed. Seek the overriding purpose in your work—there is one there somewhere. Find the transcendent cause. Work for that and your career and your life will be a success.

When you sell Royal, believe in Royal with all your heart.

Good people don't want to be managed.
They want to fight for a cause.

By the time I left Methodist, our employees numbered about 5,000. The average tenure in the organization was ten years. The *average* was *ten years*! In Houston's dynamic labor market, that was an incredibly long-tenured workforce. An employee base that large and that stable was a blessing. To those long-term employees, Methodist was more than a job, it was a career. Most of them had made a life-long commitment to caring for the sick and injured. They were intelligent, hard working, and fiercely proud of working at Methodist. They were the very best. They taught me something about leadership.

These were people who didn't need to be managed. They didn't need to be led. They were incredibly motivated, dedicated, and loyal to the institution. They were engaged in a career-long noble cause. They inspired and motivated *me*. So, what was my job as their leader?

My job was to be the champion for the cause—to define it, to promote it, to defend it, to cheer it, to praise it, and to enlist others in its service. The cause I championed—their cause—was this: "To provide the best care and service in the world." That was Methodist's mission and every employee knew it and was proud that we were trying to be the best. I know it might sound egotistical, maybe pretentious. But, let me explain how that came to be our cause.

As soon as I became CEO, the management team and I began a serious strategic planning process. The first step, as always, was to assess the organization and define its mission. In the assessment process we reached several important conclusions: Methodist was a strong organization with a history of outstanding medical and hospital care. It had a great board, volunteers, and employees. Its Sunbelt, Texas, Houston, and Texas Medical Center locations were all strengths, as was its close relationship with Baylor College of Medicine. Patients came from around the world to its first class medical staff, and because of all that, it had the opportunity to be among the best in the world.

We concluded that if we had that opportunity, then we had the obligation to try to be the best. It became our mission. My job as CEO for all those years was to paint that mission in vivid colors and do everything in my command to achieve it.

If you are fortunate enough to be a hospital executive, you will find the kind of people who are ready to fight for a cause. They are the very best people. They require little management, little leadership. But, they do require a worthy champion—a champion for the cause of caring and serving. Like a knight of old, you might want to spend the night before you accept the champion's banner in the chapel on your knees praying that you will be worthy. It is a noble cause.

It is a quantum leap from outstanding individual performer to outstanding manager. It is an even greater leap to outstanding leader of leaders.

As assistant to the president at Methodist, I was required to be an outstanding individual performer. If I wrote a speech for the president, it was expected to be a good one; if I prepared a staff analysis, it was counted upon to be complete and well thought through. When I represented the president, I was expected to be a positive reflection on him. Then, when I was promoted to first level executive, I realized that none of my individual performance skills would make me an effective leader of the department heads and individual employees assigned to me. Now, I would need to get the best performance out of others rather than from myself.

That is a leap in performance that is sometimes difficult. A common mistake in hospitals is the promotion of the best clinical nurse to head nurse, the best medical technician to laboratory manager, or the best physical therapist to department head. Unfortunately, very few of these people's clinical skills qualify them for leadership positions. While clinical competence confers respect from peers at the time of promotion, a very different set of skills is needed for success as a leader. The ability to plan, organize, control, direct, and evaluate in a fair and judicious manner; the ability to motivate and lead; and the ability to get the best out of each individual follower are the arts and skills needed in a first level - leadership position. To be effective, newly promoted managers must resist the temptation to do it themselves; they must find ways to get the job done through others—even when they know they could do it better themselves.

The leap from outstanding individual performer to manager is a big one, but the jump from there to managing senior staff is even greater. Top-level executives are different than line employees. They are leaders in their own rights, with their own concepts of leadership, their own proven methods, and their own styles. When I became a CEO, I realized that my approach to my key team members needed to be different from the one I had used as a junior executive. In recognition of the senior executives' track records of success with a variety of styles, I needed to be less directive and more collaborative. I decided to be more the coach and less the quarterback.

The lesson of this maxim is this: As you rise through the executive ranks, you should carefully think through the leadership requirements at each stage. What will make you a success as a staff analyst? What will get you promoted to department chief? What will make you a success as a department head? What will get you promoted to junior executive? What leadership skills and successes will you need to enter senior management? To become a chief executive? And, once there, what approach to your senior team will be most effective? There are nuances and differences at each level.

Management is nothing more (nor less) than people and money.

Management is nothing more than handling an organization's people and finances. That is a fairly common executive belief. And, the basic precept is correct: Manage the means of production (the people) and insure the future of the organization (make a profit) and you will be a successful executive. It sounds so easy. And, in concept, it is. Management isn't, after all, rocket science or brain surgery. Motivate and lead the people and make sure income exceeds outgo—pretty basic stuff. However, it is the idea that management is nothing *less* than people and money that is important.

Those executives who get it right understand that managing the people and the money is an infinitely complex and difficult task. They are not deluded by the fact that there are only two variables. Those who are the best, paint a vision of the future that motivates and inspires, communicate the mission clearly, and remove the barriers to success for their employees. The best executives know the financial needs of the organization, see that it is operated within appropriate financial structures, and insure profitability—the key to an organization's continued existence.

Unfortunately, there are far too few executives who get it right. Those who don't, blame the industry. They blame the lawmakers. They blame the unions. They blame the regulators. To those who say, "We are losing money because of the environment," I reply, "Somewhere in your industry, there is a company just like yours that is providing a superior product and making a profit. Why aren't you?" At Methodist, our team's attitude was this: Tell us what the rules are and, no matter how onerous, we will play by them and win.

To those of you who are playing by the rules—and they *are* onerous today in the healthcare industry—and winning, I salute you. You understand the importance of getting the people and money equation right. You have profitable organizations made up of enlightened, informed, and inspired people. Unfortunately, your brand of leadership is in the minority today.

The darkest days for an organization are those when all the base businesses are losing money; the people are dispirited, not knowing where the organization is going or what is going to happen next; and the leaders are adrift. Decisions don't get made or, if they do, they are far too late to be effective. In such a situation, I say to the chief executive, one of two things should happen. First, the business may not be viable; if so, *get out of the business.* That option is rarely available to those who run non-profit hospitals. That leaves the second option: if you've fumbled the people and the money, *get out of the corner office.* Somebody else can get it right. I guarantee it.

Credit is rarely given, often taken.

It is often said that success has many fathers, while failure is an orphan. That can be particularly true in the executive suite where credit for successful accomplishment is a valuable commodity. It brings an executive raises in pay, bonuses, promotions, and the high opinion of peers, subordinates, and superiors. Therefore, it isn't surprising that there is a constant, if subtle skirmish in the executive ranks to grab the honors for the organization's successes. Far too often, senior managers take credit rather than give it. That is a leadership mistake.

It is inherent in organizations that leaders are generally credited for successes and blamed for failures. If you preside over a successful task force or if one of your areas of responsibility hits an operational or financial home run, the organization will credit you with the success. If you preside over an effort that fails, the organization will blame you. That is as it should be. Effective leaders will have successes; they will have failures. Hopefully, the successes will both outweigh and outnumber the failures.

However, when success does come, *take no credit*—give all of the recognition to the team that did the work. When failure comes, publicly accept *all* of the blame. Credit should flow down the organizational chart, while blame should flow up. And, as a leader, you should realize that is exactly what happens: success is the team's; failure is the leader's. Handle the credit accordingly.

After integrity, perseverance is
an executive's most valuable trait.

It was October of 1941. A black-shirted wave of tyranny had swept across Europe. The Nazi panzers had brushed aside Belgium and Holland, rolled into Paris, and now France lay defeated. The United States had not yet entered the war. Against Hitler's unvanquished forces, Britain stood alone. Utterly alone.

Winston Churchill, the defiant British prime minister, carried on his stout shoulders all the weight of those terrible days. It was the low point in the Second World War for the English-speaking people. To bolster his spirits, Churchill decided to pay a visit to his old school, Harrow. On a bright October day, he drove to the school and there addressed the boys. He told them of the dire circumstances that England faced; he told them of the dark days to come and the sacrifices that would be required. And, then in words that each boy there would remember for the rest of his life, Churchill told them "Never give in. Never give in. Never. Never. Never. Never."

You know the rest of the story. The Royal Air Force defeated the Luftwaffe in the battle of Britain. The United States entered the war and joined Britain in defeating the Germans and the Japanese and saved the world from global totalitarianism.

I love that story of Churchill at Harrow. I love what it says about the indomitable spirit of that grand old lion of empire, what it says about leadership in desperate times, and what it says about perseverance.

110

Perseverance is the ability to keep at it, come what may, to hang in there, to doggedly stick with it in the face of anything and everything. For an executive, particularly one in an industry that is going through its own dark days, that trait is second only to absolute integrity. Perseverance beats brilliance every time. Perseverance beats strategy. It trumps tactics. It wears down your competition. It inspires your people.

As you face the bad times, think back to the threatening days of October of 1941 and picture that stocky figure in a black suit as he defiantly tells the boys of Harrow, "Never give in." When you think your leadership is waning, when you think the cause is lost, and when your people have lost hope, reach deep down within yourself and muster the strength to go on. As we Yanks would say, "Never give up." Never give up on your leadership. Never give up on your values. Never give up on your mission.

Never give in. Never give in. Never. Never. Never. Never.

Leadership is a privilege, a responsibility, and a burden.

Leadership is a privilege. For most young executives, the privilege part of leadership is the part first learned and the one most enjoyed. Of course, it is a privilege. As a new executive, you have been recognized as a leader. You have been promoted to executive status. You have been given rank in the organization, which sets you apart. You are now the boss. And bosses have privileges. You are no longer a slave to the time clock. You have that great new executive title. Chances are, you have your own office, your own secretary. You now have departments reporting to you. You have subordinates who look to you for leadership. You may even have new executive perquisites, such as an expense account. You are a participant in meetings that include the highest levels of executives in the organization. You may even be invited to attend a Board meeting and be introduced there. You have arrived. You are now in the executive suite and it is the executive *sweet*. You bask in it all. Leadership is a privilege.

Leadership is a responsibility. Even as you bask in your new status, the responsibility of leadership begins to extend its somber tentacles toward you. Your new secretary has a personal problem that she needs to discuss with you immediately. A new department heads informs you that there is a sexual harassment charge being made against her by an employee. That high level executive meeting you were so looking forward to? You have been placed on the agenda to present your plans to improve the financial performance of your departments, none of which have performed up to expectations in the past year. That warm glow of privilege is slowly being transformed into a cold hard knot of dread. You are learning one of the first lessons of leadership. *Noblesse oblige.* "With nobility comes responsibility." That admonition to kings is now your own. With executive leadership comes responsibility.

Leadership is a privilege. It is a responsibility. Most good executives enjoy the privilege part, but push it to the background, since exhibiting too much joy in executive status is not attractive and, in fact, can interfere with effective leadership. Likewise, most good executives accept and respond effectively to the responsibility inherent in leadership. After all, they have been trained to accept and discharge executive tasks. But, it is the truly outstanding executive who knows that to be a great organizational leader, you must understand and accept the very real *burden* of leadership.

That burden is the impact that your words, actions, and decisions can have in the lives of other human beings—your organization's employees and patients. Employees now listen to your words and not just to their literal meaning. They seek clues and hidden messages in those words. "How am I doing? Is there a layoff coming? What did you mean by that?" Countless sleepless hours have been spent in analysis of a boss' innocuous comments. The burden of clear written and oral communications is one to be taken most seriously.

Your actions are watched just as closely. "What's bothering the chief today? Did you see him? His head's down. That frown! I don't know about you, but I'm staying out of his way today." A leader's expression of anger can bruise feelings, cause organizational uneasiness, and create a tenuous relationship with subordinates—all of which interferes with effective leadership. But it is the impact of your decisions that is the greatest burden. A simple schedule change can disrupt child-care arrangements. A job reassignment can cause stress. Terminating an employee, while unpleasant for any leader, can literally be devastating for the employee, both from a career and from a life perspective. Decisions about staffing levels can threaten lives in a clinical setting. Decisions in ethically and legally murky areas can have later consequences that bring the organization to its knees. It is the best of executives who speak, act, and decide only in the context of this burden.

Being chosen to lead other human beings in important enterprises—such as in the American healthcare system—is tremendously rewarding and fulfilling. When you are there, enjoy the privileges that being the leader brings. Take your leadership responsibilities seriously. Solve problems, improve performance, build teams. But, most importantly, always carry the burden of what your words, acts, and decisions mean in the lives of others.

Career

Leadership of those who care for the sick and injured is a noble profession—well worth the investment of a career.

The five years I spent in the United States Regular Army did two things for me: It honed my leadership skills and it convinced me I didn't want to spend a career in the Army. My year in combat in Vietnam also did two things for me: It made me grateful for my life and it made me want to dedicate it to something "good." I chose to be an executive leader in the healthcare industry and it was the best decision I could have made.

The rewards are spectacular. First, there is the leadership aspect. In a modern hospital, an executive must rely upon persuasion, motivation, and inspiration to be successful; there is little raw power inherent in the executive suite. The hospital is the home of independent physicians who control the destiny of the organization by their decisions to admit and treat patients there. It is also the home of semi-independent professionals such as nurses, pharmacists, and physical therapists who answer not only to the organization but also to the higher calling of their professions. Leading these highly educated and motivated people in an organization dedicated to excellence is fulfilling and gratifying beyond belief.

The second rewarding aspect is your relationship with the people whose lives intertwine with the hospital. In addition to the physicians, nurses, and other professionals are the incredible diversity of people in the employee ranks and the patients themselves. Methodist's workforce during my years there averaged 80 percent women and 60 percent minority, with representatives of at least 30 foreign countries among them. Seeing such a diverse mix of workers striving every day *for years* to bring the best care and service to their patients was an ongoing revelation and a delight.

Our patients continued to amaze and inspire me. They came from every state in the union and from more than 80 foreign countries yearly. They included kings, sheiks, presidents, senators, congressmen, professional athletes, entertainers, business tycoons, salesmen, farmers, clerks, housewives, househusbands, laborers, the unemployed, and the homeless. They came because they were sick or injured and wanted to be healed. Their experiences ranged from miraculous cures to tragic deaths. But the good experiences far outweighed the bad and we reaped the rewards of seeing relieved, cured, and healed patients leave our ministering hands.

Healthcare is inherently "good." I know I could have been a lawyer and had a happy and productive life. If I had not gone to college, I could have been a carpenter and had a happy and productive life. But, I know that one day I will lie in a coronary care unit of one of our hospitals, and realizing it is my last illness, I will review my life. There will be things for which I am sorry; things of which I am proud. At the top of the list among the latter will be this: I am proud that I spent my career using my leadership abilities to organize and lead the marvelous people who dedicated their lives to the healing care and service of their fellow human beings.

An executive's life is a series of peaks and valleys.
The challenge is discerning whether you are
on a peak or in a valley.

One of the happiest days at the beginning of my career was when Methodist adopted corporate executive titles in the early 1970s. We had used the designations standard for hospital management—administrative assistant, assistant administrator, associate administrator, and administrator. Now, Mr. Bowen was to be president. I had just completed my administrative residency and joined the permanent staff as an administrative assistant, working specifically for him. He called me into his office and briefed me on the changes. Then he said, "There are two titles I want you to consider for yourself: Assistant Vice President or Assistant to the President." Assuming that the other administrative assistants would be given assistant vice president titles and that I alone would be ASSISTANT TO THE PRESIDENT—publicly acknowledged as the right hand of the PRESIDENT—I gladly chose that appellation. What a mountaintop feeling.

When the announcement memo was published days later, I was stunned to see that I wasn't the only assistant to the president. He had also given that title to his secretary!

Another trip to the peaks was my promotion to executive vice president and chief operating officer. At age 36, I was elevated by Mr. Bowen above all other executives at Methodist and entrusted with leadership of a much-needed financial and operations turnaround. It was the peak of Mt.

Everest. However, the three years I spent on top of the world as COO turned out to be my career's most miserable and difficult ones, as Methodist dealt with the illness and subsequent departure of its president.

Throughout my years as an executive, I had many similar experiences. So many that I always became uneasy when things were going well—good financial results, awards, good press. When we were on the peaks, I instinctively looked ahead to the valleys. Sure enough, the quick descents came.

"An investigative reporter is in the lobby and wants to interview you."

"We just got this letter from the IRS. They're coming to audit us."

"The Attorney General has just sued us."

"There's been a suicide on the psych unit."

There were many glorious climbs, many days in the clear high air among the rose-colored clouds. Wonderful. Exhilarating. It is breathtaking up there on the peaks. Unfortunately, there were also days in the shadowed depths, where uncertainty lurked, and menace extended its cold reach. Dispiriting. Depressing. It is dark down there in the valleys.

But, when you become an executive, you have signed up for the valleys. Organizations need executives *because* there are valleys. If organizations didn't have problems, didn't get into trouble, or didn't require periodic turnarounds, they would run themselves—there would be no need for executive leadership. Your reason for being *is* the depths; the heights, when and if they come, are your compensation for handling the depths. Your executive career will, if you are lucky, be a series of both peaks and valleys. What makes it truly interesting is that it is often impossible to tell at any given moment where on the path you are. A strategy that looks like a winner sucks the financial life's blood from the base business. Conversely, a challenging and difficult audit creates a better and stronger organization.

Don't spend a lot of time worrying about whether your problems and challenges will turn out to be peak or valley experiences. You won't know while you are dealing with them and, perhaps, it will be years before you truly know. But, if it seems at the moment that you are in a valley, get used to it. That is where your work is; that is where your worth is. And, if it seems at the moment that you have reached the summit, turn your face to the sun and enjoy the feeling. It won't last long before you are needed back in the valley.

*Without a sense of the appropriate,
it is almost impossible to succeed.*

Wear brown wingtips with your tux?

Appear in a mini-skirt at a board meeting?

Tell an off-color joke at a funeral?

Get drunk at the company Christmas party?

Make a pass at the boss' wife?

These are all inappropriate behaviors. They are examples of the kind of comportment that, when observed in an executive, can derail a career.

Being a successful executive has many requirements: credentials, intelligence, judgment, hard work, and luck, among others. But, without a sense of the appropriate, all of them may not be enough to bring success. It is important to know when to talk; it is important to know what to say. It is important to know how to dress appropriately for every occasion—the office, the golf course, the quail hunt, the beach party, the country weekend. Showing up in the office wearing golf cleats is as inappropriate as playing eighteen holes in an Armani suit. And, it is important to know how to act in every situation.

If you are a senior executive and you have not developed a sense of the appropriate, it is too late for you (and a wonder that you reached the senior ranks). If you are just entering the executive suite, watch carefully. What are the senior people wearing, what are they saying, how do they act? By observation and analysis, learn the appropriate behaviors for that culture. While not all executive suites are conservative places, most of them are. Keep your haircut, jewelry, grooming, dress, and behavior well within bounds. While a few outrageous mavericks have made it to the top, they are the exceptions, not the rule.

Oh, one more thing. Buy some black patent leather shoes. Ditch the mini-skirt.

When one executive is promoted, one person is happy.

In my 12-year trek from resident to president, I was promoted 6 times. During my later 14 years as a CEO, I was privileged to promote many executives. From both experiences, I concluded that, in the executive suite, when one person is promoted, only one person is happy.

Executive suites are very competitive places. Stakes can be high, because salaries, bonuses, recognition, and advancement ride on comparative performance. When outstanding performance results in promotion to a higher rank, it not only speaks volumes about the winner, it draws attention to those who were *not* promoted.

So, who are the potential happy executives when a vice president is promoted to senior vice president? Former peers? No. All of the vice presidents who are not moved up are, of course, downright unhappy. The promotion of one of their rank, leaving them behind, is a powerful negative message about their comparative performance. New peers? No. The senior vice presidents will not welcome the new arrival with open arms. Their ranks have been increased by a new rival. Superiors? No. The executive vice presidents will not be pleased to see a new rising star in the organization: "Will this hot shot take my job?" Subordinates? No. The younger executives will not be thrilled that senior management ranks have just increased: "There's another senior VP I'll have to wade through to get to the top."

The only happy person in the executive suite is the newly minted senior vice president. If you find yourself in a similar happy circumstance, remember that behind all the congratulations and best wishes there is considerable discontent. Because of that, you should make an effort to tone down the wattage of your grin and limit public displays of self-satisfaction. That will be hard to do. After all, you are the hot shot who just got promoted; you are the new member of senior management. But, if you want the *next* promotion, you are going to need the help and cooperation of those peers, subordinates, and superiors of yours, all of whom are decidedly less elated than you are with the blessed event. Now is a great time for modesty and true expressions of gratitude to those who have made you successful.

Be nice to everyone on the way up.
You will need them on the way down.

There are two messages in this maxim. The first is the admonition to behave in a pleasant and appropriate manner as you rise in the organization. That is an important message, but more important is the second: What goes up must come down.

Being "nice" to people in the organization means treating them as fellow and equal human beings, appreciating them for their contributions, thanking them, smiling at them, and speaking civilly and pleasantly with them. Doing so pays dividends. You make friends and allies at all levels of the organization; you create reservoirs of good will for yourself. And such reservoirs of good will are absolutely essential for effective leadership, particularly when times turn tough—as they always do. Unfortunately, executives often are too busy or too stressed or too something to be nice to the people around them. Their leadership is diminished because of it.

It may help you, as it did me, to remember to be nice to people in the organization if you will remind yourself of the second part: If I rise, I will fall. It is an absolute certainty that you will not be on top forever. You will one day leave the lofty eagle's aerie of the corner office. You may glide gracefully to earth in your own time and at your own pace or you may be shot down in mid-flight. Either way, you *will* come down. When you do, you will leave two legacies. One will be the performance of your organization during your watch; the second will be the relationship you had with your fellow human beings who, along with you, tied their lives to the enterprise.

Jerry Glanville, a former head coach of the now defunct Houston Oilers, said, "We are only coaches in the national football league for an eye blink." He knew that no matter how long one coached, when it was over it would seem incredibly brief. The same can be said for tenure as a chief executive. My own 14 years in the CEO chair were only the blink of an eye. While I was there, I constantly reminded myself that someday it would be over, and when it was, I wanted a reservoir of friendship and good will from the people with whom I spent so many years. So, be nice! It's only for an eye blink.

Criticism: No one appreciates it—constructive or not.

Throughout most of my years in the CEO job, I had three senior executives, two staff executives, and my tenured executive secretary reporting directly to me. Methodist's compensation system required an annual, year-end performance evaluation of direct reports. On a scale of 1 to 4 (4 being the best), every year I ranked each one of them a 4 in every evaluation category. In the comments section of each form, I praised them for their great contributions during the past year and emphasized their value to our organization and to me as a leader. I never wrote a critical remark. I never wrote a suggestion for improvement.

To many veterans of the executive suite, that will seem odd, if not downright bad, management practice. I can hear the reactions now, "How does that develop people? How does it improve performance?" My reasons for doing evaluations in this manner arose from my personal experience and from my observations of evaluation systems in both the military and in the executive suite. I personally detested even the slightest criticism or suggestion for improvement from above. I was always harder on my own performance than any of my bosses were and I never liked to hear it from them while I was taking myself to task. I knew better than they did where I might have done better and how I could improve. Also, I have repeatedly observed the anger, resentment, disappointment, frustration, and occasionally, tears, over performance evaluations that included "constructive" criticism. For motivated, professional people, criticism is not comfortable or desirable.

Executives have worked long and hard to obtain the necessary advanced academic degrees to qualify as leaders. They are, by and large, intelligent, hard-working, dedicated, and motivated. After a while in the organization, they have a track record of success. If they didn't, they would not still be there. They have strong egos. If they didn't, they probably would not be executives. They are proud.

The team that reported to me was like that. They were senior, tenured people. They were accomplished. I believed they were the best in the organization, maybe the best in the industry. And, if they were the best, they deserved the best ratings.

Criticism, even the "constructive" kind, can cause misunderstandings, mistrust, and resentment; it can sour the relationship between leaders and subordinates. In the upper reaches of management, praise works much better. It reinforces good behavior and it creates a bond of good will. A simple absence of praise is more than enough to let an executive know that there is room for improvement.

I do not necessarily recommend that my performance evaluation philosophy be used in all cases. It probably does, in fact, fail to measure up as a good management practice. But, it worked for me—as a good *leadership* practice.

The challenge is not in finding a mentor.
It's knowing when to change mentors.

Kindergarten teacher. Fifth grade teacher. Debate coach. Senior English teacher. Night editor. ROTC instructor. Professor of Military Science. Healthcare administration program director. President of The Methodist Hospital. President of Lufkin Memorial Hospital. Chairman of the board of Methodist. All of these people took a special interest in me at one stage of my life or other and they all had a significant impact on my future career. They were my mentors.

But mentors in an organizational setting are different from ones in other aspects of your life. In the organizational setting, your mentors identify and define you. They can make your career and they can break your career. If you want to rise in the organization, hitch up to a rising star above you. If you become this star's protégé, you will rise with him or her. When I became chief operating officer, my former vice presidents in my division became my new senior vice presidents. When I was named chief executive officer, they became my executive vice presidents. They rose with me. But, what happens when the star is no longer rising in the organization?

When Methodist's president, Ted Bowen, abruptly retired, I was his number-two executive. All of my subordinates believed I would be named to replace him. Instead, the board selected its chairman, A. Frank Smith, Jr., as interim president and launched a national search for Bowen's successor. The search lasted nine months. During that miserable interlude, there were many times that my chances to be that successor looked pretty slim. Ted Bowen had been my mentor. Now he was gone. But, over those months, Frank Smith became my friend and mentor. While I was going through the process of winning the job and changing mentors, my key lieutenants faced many uncertain moments. Had tying their careers to mine been a mistake? Would they lose if I did? What would happen to them if an outside CEO were named? Should they sever their close ties to me? It was a time of great uncertainty for all of us. From a career standpoint, it was a time of danger.

If you want to rise in the executive hierarchy, find a patron in the organization above you. It should be someone who is a good bet to be a rising star—a winner. Get on that person's team and rise with him or her. But, if your mentor turns out to be a falling star, find a new one rising. If both your old mentor and your new mentor are still in your organization, know that you are in a dangerous position. Your old mentor could very well turn on you and possibly damage your organizational standing and, perhaps, your career. Your new patron may not be able to protect you.

Finding a mentor is the easy part. Changing mentors requires finesse, tact, and skill. Even with the ultimate in diplomacy, it can fail. So, as you follow that star, do everything to make it shine brightly. You have a huge stake in its rise. And, if it falls or burns out, realize the tenuousness of your position. Carefully, alter your orbit to another star. Carefully, because stars are suns and suns can burn you.

What do you want to be, good at your present job or
promoted? You won't rise in the organization
by being good at your present job; you get promoted
by demonstrating your ability to do the job above. All
being good at your present job does is make you tired.

It is provocative to say this. And, of course, I say it with tongue in cheek. But, superior performance in any executive position does require an unusual degree of effort. Long hours and hard work usually add up to superior performance and long hours and hard work can wear you out. But, outstanding work in your present job is not the primary criterion for your next move up the corporate ladder. For one thing, worn out executives do not make attractive candidates for promotion.

Sadly, in many organizations there are managers and executives who are so good at their important jobs that they don't get promoted. They literally make themselves indispensable to their present jobs. Being proficient at your job is not a bad thing. Obviously, it makes a contribution to the organization. It keeps you employed. It keeps the salary and benefits rolling in. And it is, in fact, assumed that you will have performed well in your present assignment when you are under consideration for promotion. It just isn't the criterion upon which the promotion decision will be made.

Promotion comes to executives who best demonstrate, in their present jobs, the abilities and traits required for the higher position.   The highest rated executive in an organization, say a vice president for purchasing, won't necessarily be chosen COO.   The executive in the organization who has demonstrated the best leadership skills and the toughest hide will be named.   There are almost always more than one candidate for promotion, sometimes insiders and outsiders.   Each candidate will be assumed to be performing well; the one selected will be the one with the obvious abilities and traits needed in the higher slot.

So, if you are in an executive position and want to move up, what do you do?   First, study the position you want carefully.   What is needed in that job?   What kind of leadership?   What kind of credentials?   What kind of knowledge?.   Then, obtain the necessary credentials and knowledge and, in your present job, demonstrate the brand of leadership needed.   Second, study the individual or group who will make the selection.   How do they make decisions?   What traits are they likely to emphasize?   Build those into your current job performance.   Third, try to anticipate the impact of the organization's history and the industry's environment.   An organization that has had a lawyer as CEO, may be ready for an operations person as chief.   A tough industry financial climate may boost the chief financial officer into the corner office.   Fourth, groom someone under you to take your current job and constantly sing that person's praises and readiness to rise in the organization.

Finally, do your job well, but don't become indispensable.   And don't let it exhaust you.   You won't think as well or look as good at the promotion interview.

Tracks are only fast when viewed in retrospect.

As a speaker, I have been introduced on more than one occasion, by someone who referred to my "fast-track" career, saying something like, "he rose from resident to president in just 12 short years." When I hear that, I just shake my head. When I was running on that track, it didn't look or feel so fast. In the actual running, it was a long, slow, hard, uphill pull.

Before becoming president and chief executive officer, I served one year as a resident, two years as assistant to the president, four years as a vice president, two years as a senior vice president, and three years as executive vice president and COO. Those years were filled with long, long hours, challenging problems, and many sacrifices. I was not as involved in my daughters' activities as I should have been. I never took all the vacation time I was entitled to. On many holidays, I spent part of the day at Methodist. It wasn't unusual to begin my day with a breakfast meeting and end it with a dinner meeting. And along the way came heart attacks and surgeries. During those years, I did not have what is commonly referred to today as a "balanced life."

But, I do not regret the race. If you are on the "fast track," know that it will not look or feel like that in the running. It is only at the finish line that you and others will see that it was. Know, too, that along with the race itself, there will be personal and family costs. If you are not prepared to pay them as you run, step off the track. Others will be willing to pay those costs and they are only a step behind. The race I ran took 12 years; by anyone's standard, 12 years is not a short time. If you think it is, imagine it in another context—say, the time from first to twelfth grades. It was more like a marathon than a sprint. I ran it as well as I could, paid the price along the way, and won. The chance to lead was my gold medal. It was worth the race.

For promotion to senior management, good credentials, hard work, outstanding performance, and good grooming are all givens. Selection is based on fit with others at the top.

There is a huge pool of executives to choose from for positions in senior management in organizations. And, those executives are qualified for those positions. Almost all final candidates for selection at the top will have impeccable credentials. They have gone to the right schools and done well there. They have demonstrated their ability to work hard and have a history of outstanding executive performance. They will be well dressed and well groomed. So, if all the candidates for the very highest levels of an organization possess all that, how is one of them selected?

The successful candidate for senior management is the one who is deemed to be the best fit with others at the top. He is the individual with whom the other members of the senior team feel most comfortable. And all too often, the use of the masculine pronoun in that sentence is, for women executives, an unfortunate statement of fact.

In the healthcare industry, as well as corporate America, the upper echelons of organizational leadership are filled predominately with middle-aged, white men. They are the gatekeepers to the corner office and to those closest to it. Their conversations are often about golf, team sports, hunting, and, for some of the older ones, the military—subjects in which most women executives are not usually well versed. More often than not, the keys to the executive suite are handed to another well-qualified middle-aged, white man—not the equally well-qualified woman. "He just seems like a better fit with the team."

If you are committed to climbing the corporate ladder all the way to the top, there are lessons here for both male and female executives. Know that there is going to be formidable competition from a large number of highly qualified candidates, all of whom want that last rung just as badly as you do. So, first, see to your credentials, performance, appearance, and demeanor. They all must to be sterling just to get you a chance at the top. Next, come to terms with the "fit" issue. It is not unreasonable to place importance upon fit. You will spend more time, and in more stressful situations, with the other members of senior management than you will with your spouse, your kids, or your friends. Comfort with one another is important. It is important for the team as a whole, but it is important for you as well. You don't want to spend your work life uncomfortable, mismatched with other senior executives. Carefully evaluate how the team will accept and work with you and, just as importantly, evaluate how you will accept and work with them. Do not accept a position that isn't a fit for both.

If you are a woman executive, the message is not all negative. There are more women in senior management today than there were ten years ago. There are more women hospital and healthcare system CEOs today than there were ten years ago. The graduate schools of healthcare management now train more women executives than men. As those graduates move into middle management, then into the executive ranks, the dynamics will change. I can speculate that a senior management team made up entirely of women would find a woman to be the best fit as an addition to the group. However, I can hope that a senior management made up entirely of women would find the best fit as an addition to the team, without regard to gender. I hope you will be better than we were.

Credentials: They don't guarantee you success, but they demonstrate that you are serious and will work hard to succeed.

My senior management team and I spent a considerable amount of time thinking through the issue of academic credentials. Some team members had advanced professional degrees, some didn't. At issue was whether our policies would require advanced degrees for promotion to middle management and the executive ranks. Those who argued against such a requirement pointed out numerous examples of successful Methodist leaders who didn't have advanced degrees. They advocated experience and a track record of success. Those who supported the prerequisite advocated professionalism and argued that, since we required an all board-certified medical staff, how could we lead with a management staff that was less than fully qualified? The policy we established required all *newly hired* or *promoted* middle managers or executives to possess experience, a track record of success, *and* the appropriate advanced professional degree.

If you are going to build a career commitment to a profession—particularly one as important as leading organizations that make a life-and-death difference in people's lives every day—then lay a proper foundation. Advanced degrees in healthcare management, business administration, public health, or law form a solid foundation upon which to build. A degree itself, of course, does not insure career success, but it can speak eloquently. As a CEO who hired many young people just entering the profession, it said something to me. When I saw an individual with a strong grade point average from an excellent professional program, it said: "Here is a person who respects *my* profession; she has taken her career seriously by choosing an excellent school and has shown, through academic performance, that she will work hard to succeed. I can bet on somebody who starts off like that."

The effectiveness of an association is inversely related to the diversity of its membership.

During my career, I was active on the boards of the associations that represent the healthcare industry. It was an honor and a privilege for me to serve and lead the Greater Houston Hospital Council, the Texas Hospital Association, the American Hospital Association, and the American College of Healthcare Executives. I believed that was a productive use of my time, and that it would benefit my organization, because those associations took positions with regulators and legislators whose work affected Methodist. I respected and admired the associations' leaders and staff, but I came to see the weakness of those organizations as advocates for the industry.

You have heard that a rose is a rose is a rose. A hospital is not a hospital is not a hospital. There are for-profit and not-for-profit hospitals. There are Protestant and Catholic hospitals. Urban and rural hospitals. Small and large hospitals. Teaching and community hospitals. And public, psychiatric, veterans and children's hospitals. Each of these different types of institutions has its own special set of regulatory and legislative priorities. Many times their priorities are in conflict with those of other types of hospitals. When conflicting priorities involve the flow of state or federal dollars, the advocacy of the hospital association is neutralized. When there are financial winners and losers, all the association can do is moderate both gains and losses—not a very palatable solution for either the winners or the losers. The more diverse the membership, the less effective the advocacy of the association.

The most effective advocacy association I worked with was the Association of Academic Medical Centers' Council of Teaching Hospitals. Its membership had very similar characteristics and priorities—medical education and research. The Council's advocacy agenda was, therefore, very specific and very targeted. It was a rifle while the state and national hospital associations were shotguns.

During your career, you will have to deal with your industry's associations, or at least the results of their advocacy positions. I would encourage you to become active in your state and national organizations. They are great places to meet the industry leaders, to network, and to learn what works and what doesn't in other markets. But, don't rely solely on a state or national association to advance your corporation's regulatory or legislative agenda. Have your own advocacy people and agenda. If you rely on associations exclusively, you can find your positions compromised by the diversity of their members' conflicting interests.

It's tough to stay in one organization for your entire career—you have to live with your results.

I spent my entire executive career at Methodist in Houston. I did that by design. It was the only place I wanted to work; it was the only place I wanted to lead. I never allowed my name to be used by executive recruiters in their searches for other organizations. Of my twenty-six years there, nineteen were spent in senior management: two as senior VP, three as COO, and fourteen as CEO. During those years I formulated policies and procedures and implemented strategies that shaped and guided the institution. Knowing that I would spend my career there and would have to live with and implement my decisions brought an extra degree of deliberation to the decision-making process. But, I have to confess, I sometimes looked enviously at my colleagues in the industry who moved to new organizations every few years.

It *is* easier to lead when you are new to your position and are in the assessment phase of a job. You have everyone's attention; there is excitement about the possibilities a new leader brings. Simply announcing new strategies and tactics causes an initial burst of enthusiasm and hope for the future. If you depart in this phase—within three to five years—you really haven't been tried. At your next stop, you are back in the exciting first phase again.

But the executive who moves from organization to organization does not necessarily have it easier than the one who stays put. You face a whole array of new problems and

143

new faces at each stop. You must sort out the players, learn the community, assess the strategy, and set your course for the organization. Those are formidable tasks. But, knowing that you will depart in a few short years changes the dimensions of those tasks. The pressure to get those decisions right is reduced, if you know you will not have to permanently face the people affected or be responsible for the long-term implementation and implications of your strategic decisions.

Those who stay and rise from inside, get the excitement of the assessment and new direction phase. But, staying means you also get the long, up-hill slog of operationalizing your decisions. You must face the inevitable performance glitches, people problems, and unforeseen consequences. Plus, you are identified in neon lights as the author of the decisions and you publicly carry the credit or the blame for the success or failure of their execution.

Stay in one organization or job hop? Either is an acceptable way to manage your career. But, if you move around, try to make your decisions at each stop as if *you* are the one who will see them through to completion. Hospitals, with their missions of caring and healing, deserve nothing less.

The pursuit of excellence is its own reward.

From the time I returned from the war in Vietnam and began graduate studies, I vowed to be the very best I could be. I believed that life was too short to do anything less than pursue excellence in my chosen career. I may have come up short, time and time again, but I never stopped striving for excellence. The knowledge that I always pursued it was a comfort to me. Now, at the end of my executive career, I can honestly say that I would have done it all without pay—a career of excellence in leadership is reward enough.

If you are in an executive position, you should strive for excellence in everything that you do. Because you are an executive, you and the world know that you have intelligence and capability. If you have the opportunity to be excellent, then you have the obligation to try. Leadership demands excellence. Your organization demands it. Your people demand it. And, while excellence usually brings material rewards, they pale beside the self-gratification you will receive from knowing you did it right.

Remember, life *is* short. And, if it's worth doing, it's worth doing well.

Plan the end of your career as carefully as its beginning.

George Washington is rightly called the father of his country. As commander of the Continental Army, he defeated the British forces, thus freeing the colonies to create their own destiny. As presiding officer of the Constitutional Convention, his influence was immeasurable in the adoption of the Constitution. He was *unanimously* elected the first President of the new country and, after his first term, he was *unanimously* re-elected. Without Washington, the colonies might not have gained their independence and the United States might not have been born. He is rightly revered for his outstanding leadership and statesmanship.

There is another reason to admire him—the way he left office. During his two terms, there was a movement to name him President for life. Some even proposed to crown him King. At the very least, he could accept a third term as President. With all the accomplishments and all the adulation, a lesser man might have stayed. He might have accepted appointment as President for life—even the crown of a King. Washington declined. He said his goodbyes to the Republic; he said his goodbyes to his staff. In his manner of leaving, he ennobled forever the motto on his personal seal: *finis coronat opus.* The end crowns the work.

Most executives put significant amounts of time into planning their careers. They give special thought and analysis to its beginning: what graduate school to attend, what fellowship, residency, or management development program to seek, and what starting position to take. During the climb up the executive ladder, they plan for each promotion and agonize over changing organizations. Because of that, I am always surprised at how many executives—whose profession it is to plan and to manage—end their careers in a poorly thought-out and unmanaged way.

When it comes time to depart, what are your options?

- Die in office.
- Get fired.
- Quit.
- Plan and manage your own exit.

While there is room for considerable nuance among these—forced to resign, eased out, merged out, etc.—they are basically your only departure options. Dying in office is one way to avoid the pitfalls of retirement, but it is not recommended. Getting fired is no way to end an executive career, but for far too many executives, that is the last career event. Only a fool would just quit the executive suite to end his work life. That leaves planning and managing your own exit. Why don't more executives do that?

First, they haven't really thought it through. It's a little like executives and their personal financial management; they are just too busy to take care of it. They're just too busy to think about retirement. Second, they haven't really tried to conceive of their lives after work; they haven't carefully examined their egos, their marriages, their non-work interests to know if they can successfully transition to another life. Finally, far too many have failed to provide for their financial security after the executive suite.

This was my experience with leaving the executive world: First, I had a plan. I had promised myself from the time of my mother's death at age 54 that I would not work after age 55. I saw no virtue in dying in my office; I wanted some of my life to be spent away from the stresses and strains of organizational leadership, doing things that interested me. I wanted a time while I was still fairly young, that I—not the corporation—would be in charge of me. Fifty-five was an arbitrary age to retire, but it made me focus on a date and prepare for it. The plan had an after-job activity and interests component and a financial component. But, before I got to those, I did some serious conceptual thinking. In a proposed merger with St. Luke's Episcopal Hospital, it was clear that neither side would accept the CEO of the other as leader of the combined entity. The merger was the right thing to do, but before I signed on to that, I had to confront all the ego issues. I was 52 years old, at the height of my energies and capabilities, and an industry leader. Could I leave the CEO job then? What would it mean? What would I do? After two weeks of introspection, I concluded I could leave it and, in some important personal ways, it would be liberating. The merger failed, but I had faced the concept of leaving.

The after-job activities part of the plan required some time to arrange. It is best worked out while you are still on the job. I prepared what I called a "five-year glide path." I knew that the worst scenario would be to leave the hustle and whirl of the CEO life and do nothing. Many who retire to a life of nothing to do, do not, in fact, live long. I accepted a few board positions that interested me, but not so many that I would be in continuous meetings. I decided I would write this book. I arranged to consult with boards and CEOs through my wife's consulting firm, and I decided to spend time as never before taking care of my health. Diane and I made a list of major travels to undertake. If I wanted to have absolutely nothing to do, it would take me five years from the day I left the corner office to be totally uncommitted. I swore three things:

I will not retire; I will just restructure my life.

I will not do anything that reminds me of "work."

I will not do anything just for money.

Which brings me to money. It, too, must be planned for and managed to insure financial freedom and security after employment. First, when I became an executive, I vowed never to live up to the level of my income. I always, from the very beginning, fully funded my tax-sheltered annuity and other retirement accounts. I did not buy boats, airplanes, or beach houses—things that eat money—I saved and invested conservatively. During my career, and long before I neared my transition date, I worked with my board and its compensation committee to arrange for final compensation for my chief lieutenants and for me. When the day came, there were no hurried financial arrangements and no last-minute money disputes.

Your life after the executive suite should be rich, long, and interesting. It should begin with an appropriate and dignified departure from your organization. You are the one who must see to that; you cannot rely on your boss or your board to handle it for you. If you want it done satisfactorily to you, you must pick the date and manner of your going. You must carefully examine your psyche and your ego to identify and work through retirement issues such as loss of identity, status, and self-worth that sometimes arise with the departure from executive status. You should have the elements of your life after work in place and, hopefully, a financial plan that will support that rich, long, and interesting life following your career in organizational leadership.

Your whole career and its distinguished accomplishments have been built upon your ability to plan, manage, and lead. At the end of your professional life, a poorly planned and unmanaged departure could be a tragedy—

or at minimum, a bitter experience that taints a successful career. Just like any other aspect of your executive responsibilities, face the issue, take charge of it, plan it, and execute it. Execute it with style and grace. Like Washington, let the end crown the work. It is, after all, your last executive act. Make it a class one.

CEO

The CEO is responsible for all
his organization does or fails to do.

One of the first lessons a young infantry officer is taught is this: "A commander is responsible for all his unit does or fails to do." If the platoon takes the objective in the attack, the commander is accountable; if the platoon fails and is slaughtered, he is likewise responsible. An infantry platoon is about 30 men; its commander is a lieutenant. In a unit that size, it is easy to see the relationship between leadership and responsibility: The lieutenant can almost direct the actions of each of his men. But, the mandate also applies to battalions, brigades, divisions, corps, and armies. As the lieutenant is responsible for all his platoon does or fails to do, the commanding general is held accountable for all his army does or fails to do. It is an all-encompassing and unforgiving standard.

It is a standard that I believe should apply to chief executive officers. Obviously, being responsible does not mean that a leader can control every aspect of his organization's performance; it does not even mean that a leader will necessarily know everything he needs to know about his organization to affect success or failure. But what it does mean is that the leader has developed a *proprietary* attitude toward his organization and personally accepts responsibility for its performance. I adopted that standard for my tenure in the corner office.

"What would I do if Methodist were mine? If I were its sole owner, how would I lead? Would I do things differently?" These were questions I asked myself, as I became a CEO. The answers did lead me to do things differently. First, I wanted a very personal and direct relationship with the people who daily created our success or failure—our employees. I began a series of "all employee" meetings so that I could personally spell out our mission and my expectations for our performance. I wouldn't be there at each service "moment of truth" when an employee interacted, for better or for worse, with one of our patients or one of our physicians. But, I held myself responsible for each one of those "moments of truth." Twice a year throughout my tenure, I personally faced all of Methodist's employees to emphasize our commitment to the best patient care and service. As a result of those meetings, employees felt they knew me; they knew my face, they had heard me speak passionately about our service mission. I wanted to encourage that personal relationship between the "owner" and the custodians of our mission: As I walked the halls of Methodist, no matter how preoccupied I was, I kept my head up and spoke cheerfully to each employee I saw. And, as any proprietor might, when I saw a scrap of paper or other trash in those halls, I picked it up and discarded it.

Holding myself personally accountable for all my organization did or failed to do was not an easy task. I spent many wakeful, worrying nights grappling with problems I knew I, personally, could not solve. In an institution employing thousands of people, there were murders, suicides, robberies, thefts, illegal drug use, legal drug abuse, and alcoholism—all leading to consequences. I worried about them all. A critical newspaper story cut me to the quick; a negatively slanted TV piece was a personal affront. My chairman, Frank Smith, would tell me, "Don't take these things so personally." He was afraid that I would ruin my health by doing so. He was probably right.

However, if you are chosen to be the leader of a healthcare organization, you must know two things. First, such a position is a sacred trust. Second, you will not be in it long. While there, that trust deserves all of your ability, all of your energies, and all of your *proprietary* attention and concern.

I don't care for the remote CEOs, the ones who speak to no one as they move about the organization, who communicate predominately through memos and e-mail, the ones who are not personally and passionately wedded to the results of everything their organization does or fails to do. Embracing this kind of accountability took its toll on me physically and mentally, but I am convinced that the organization performed better because I took it all so personally.

If you are relying on me for all the answers,
we are in big trouble.

I took my seat at the head of the long mahogany table in the richly paneled boardroom. It was my first meeting as a brand new chief executive officer with Methodist's executives. Having worked with them for my twelve years in the organization, I knew all these people well. I began by thanking them for the support they had given me as their chief operating officer. Then I carefully laid out my expectations for the organization during my tenure as CEO. At the very end, I told them one last thing: "If you are relying on me for all the answers, we are in big trouble."

I was succeeding a man who was a very strong, authoritarian chief. The executive team had worked under him for years and was used to his sole decision-maker style. What I was telling them was that my style would be different; I would expect them to be more responsible and more accountable, because I knew that I didn't have the knowledge, the ability, or the experience to have all the answers or make all the decisions. And, because of that, if they continued to work in the old style, the organization was not going to do well—it, we, and I would be in big trouble.

At that stage in my career, a newly minted 40-year old CEO, I was extremely self-confidant. I had risen through the organization, from resident to president, in 12 years. I had a track record of success and believed that I could do anything I set out to do in the healthcare industry. But, I also realized that an organization as large, complex, and as successful as Methodist required much, much more than my skills and intellect alone. It not only required more, it deserved more. Through the years, that proved true time and time again.

No matter how bright you are, no matter how lucky you are, and no matter how confidant you are, as CEO you alone are no match for the corporation (especially a hospital or health system). It requires the very best thinking, the hardest work, and the cooperation of every member of the team to achieve truly outstanding results. So, though you are proud, smart, and sure of yourself when you don the chief's mantle, pause before you set the tone for the tribe. Let them know that the best efforts of all the Indians and all the chiefs will be required. The tribe deserves nothing less.

On the truth: No one really wants to hear the truth.
More on the truth: The last time I heard it
was the day before I become CEO.

The unvarnished truth is a very rare commodity in corporate organizations. There are reasons people don't tell the plain truth; there are reasons people don't want to hear it. And, the higher up the organization you climb, the less likely you will hear the truth. In fact, the last time I heard it was the day before I became the CEO.

In organizations, as in society in general, people do not tell the plain truth for a variety of reasons. They pursue their own best interests. When employees must discuss something with a superior that might affect their self-interest, they will shade the discussion so that it will benefit them. If an employee is accused of something, he will present the facts in a way that protects himself. If she must deliver bad news to her boss, she will try to dampen its impact. Employees know that organizations are strewn with the dead bodies and dead careers of the bearers of bad news.

Similarly, people don't like to hear the blatant truth. It can be unpleasant. The truth about a colleague, a boss, a situation, or a snafu can create real problems. Just knowing the truth can put you in serious conflict about what to do with it. Do you confront the person about the situation? Do you report it to the boss? To the authorities? Do you just keep quiet? If you don't act, will you be in trouble when the truth comes out?

As the level of interaction rises up the organizational chart, the more the truth is tinted, shaded, and spun. The stakes get higher. Upper-level executives have the power to allocate resources, to promote, to increase compensation, and to affect careers. And, they have the power to punish. When it gets to the CEO level, the stakes are the very highest.

As I became a CEO, I was amazed at how employees handled the truth in my presence. I quickly learned never to believe at face value the first version I heard in a disputed matter. Never. There was always a different side of the "truth" to be uncovered. I also learned never to believe at face value the second side I heard. Never. I came to realize that the truth is much more complex than what one individual might report. I developed the habit of looking closely for motivations and personal interests that might be coloring the truth.

I was surprised at how difficult it was for people to deliver bad news to the CEO and how it tended to be delivered in segments, over time. I rarely got all of it at once and right between the eyes. And, I was surprised at how my natural instinct was to dislike hearing bad news. I realized I needed to hear it and as soon as possible, in order to be prepared to deal with it. But, I didn't like it.

As an executive, know that you will rarely hear the whole story. When you hear parts of it, the teller of it will be including his interpretation, which will favor him in some way. You should confront your own attitudes about hearing and dealing with the unvarnished truth. If you don't like hearing bad news, work consciously to overcome it. Avoid the temptation to "unknow" the truth. Some executives suppress difficult knowledge—almost convincing themselves they don't really know it. That is particularly dangerous, because it delays actions that should be taken to deal with difficult situations. And, avoid the trap of always believing the last person who talks to you. It is a common executive failing.

Remind yourself that, at the top of the organization, the naked truth is often clothed in shaded veils. That is the truth!

*Thank everyone. It's good manners
and it's good business.*

When I became CEO, I wanted to protect my line operating executives from the numerous requests for information and analysis that I knew I would necessarily make. While I had been a rising executive, such demands from above—for data, position papers, and the like—had been a constant distraction from my job of leading my units. I wanted my lieutenants spared that; I wanted them to be full-time leaders. The solution was the creation of the CEO Staff Services office.

Led superbly by David Huffstutler, it included two master's degree analysts and two secretaries. Their task was to handle the personal staff needs of the president, such things as speeches, data analysis, position papers, and special projects. We established rigorous procedures for handling my office correspondence. Every letter I received was answered within 24 hours. If it was something that required more time for a definitive answer, within 24 hours a letter left our offices saying we had received the correspondence, we were looking into it, and we would be back in touch when we had the answer. We created a tickler system to insure follow-up. But, what really made a difference was our policy of thanking and congratulating people.

Our staff services team and I went out of our way to find people to thank and congratulate. Employees who received any kind of recognition, whether on the job or in the community, received a letter from me praising their accomplishments and thanking them for being a credit to Methodist. We gave out Presidential Citations for Methodist employees who went above and beyond the call of duty. If a colleague in the industry—locally, in Texas, or nationally—received recognition, a letter went out. Every year, thousands of letters of thanks and congratulations poured from Methodist.

Our staff systems weren't the only means of recognizing and thanking people. We built it into our executives' and my agendas. Whenever we could, we appeared in person to thank our employee teams and units for special accomplishments or jobs extraordinarily well done.

I've heard someone call this way of thinking and acting "an attitude of gratitude."

Maybe that came from the pulpit; I don't recall. But, there is surely something to it. Too many executives get full of themselves and their own accomplishments. They forget how much a word of thanks or congratulations from them can mean to someone working their heart out in the organization or someone striving to be a better leader in a hospital. Whether you are a beginning executive or a seasoned chief executive officer, adopt an attitude of gratitude. Build thanks and congratulations into your daily schedule and develop fail-safe systems for praise and recognition of others. Your organization will be better for it. You will be a better leader for it. You will be a better person for it.

As CEO, you can do others' jobs.
No one but you can do yours.

I know of a hospital CEO who, in a snowstorm, mounted a snowplow and cleared the parking lots. Many employees thought well of him for rolling up his sleeves and braving the elements to work for the organization in a time of crisis. I'm sure he felt good about himself, too. But, when I learned of this, I wondered: While he *worked* for his organization in that emergency, who *thought* for it? Who planned for it? Who led it?

Chief executive officers are like most of us in organizations. They prefer to do the easy things, the fun things in their jobs. They like to zero in on what they know, issues that are comfortable for them, and problems that have apparent answers. Unfortunately, while CEOs are so engaged, their more difficult responsibilities are not being handled. And, also unfortunately, while any number of different people in the organization can do the easy tasks, only one person can do the CEO's.

Strategy. Policy. Change. Leadership. These are your main responsibilities as the chief. You must set strategies to accomplish the institution's vision and mission; you must formulate policies to guide its operations and activities; you must orchestrate the processes of change; and you must lead it. These are not easy tasks. They hold no certainty; they offer no clear solutions. And, they are exclusively the province of the chief executive officer. No subordinate officer can assume authority and responsibility for them. All of your time, energy, thought, and action must be focused on these critical elements of organizational success or failure. Any time spent on other elements of organizational performance, is time stolen from the tasks only the chief can do.

As an executive, you are never too good nor too high to perform any task for the organization. But, if you are tempted to sweep the floors; if you feel compelled to delve deeply into some department's operations; or, if you think you need to snowplow the parking lot, think again. While you are busy wielding the broom, stirring up the laboratory, or riding that plow, nobody is doing your job. And, the organization suffers for it.

You can have good press or bad press.
Good press is better. Don't believe either.

I *knew* I was in trouble five minutes into the interview when the young reporter told me she was new to journalism and the article she was doing was going to be a "balanced" piece. I had learned the hard way this is journalese for "hatchet job." Following the resolution of Methodist's eight-year skirmish with the Texas Attorney General, our Public Relations folks thought it would be a good idea to have me profiled in the *Wall Street Journal*. They wanted some upbeat publicity. They didn't get it. The inexperienced reporter came with a preconceived idea of the story line: "Mathis slow to bring Methodist into managed care." Unable to find physicians or competitors who would give her the negative quotes she needed for her story line, she decided to use her own devices. She wrote that I was a "troglodyte." She didn't quote someone calling me that; she simply said I was one. Naturally, the headline writer picked up on the theme and put "troglodyte" in the headline. Along with a very unattractive picture, my profile in the *Journal* was as a throwback, a caveman.

I took the stack of magazines that had accumulated on the corner of my desk and plopped them into my briefcase. It was Friday afternoon and I was loading up work and reading material for the weekend. I didn't get to the magazines until Sunday morning. The second one I came to was Business Week. The cover story was on the quality of management in not-for-profit organizations: "SURPRISE! Some of America's best-run organizations are nonprofits. Here's how corporate

America can learn from them." That caught my attention. I had always believed that the management of not-for-profit hospitals was one of the toughest leadership challenges for executives (an assessment shared by management expert Peter Drucker). Then my eyes dropped to a box in the middle of the page. It was headed, "The Best Managers, Health Services." The second of the five names listed was "Larry L. Mathis, 46, Methodist Hospital, Houston." Wow! Business Week thought I was one of the five best healthcare managers in America.

Troglodyte? Or, one of the five best in America? All things considered, I prefer the latter.

Twice I have had my picture on the cover of *Modern Healthcare*. The first time, my smiling face consumed almost all of the cover. It was superimposed on a field of blue, which matched the color of my eyes. The headline trumpeted, "Tough economy fails to stifle building boom in Houston." The article was a glowing piece on Methodist's farsighted building plans and me. The second time, it was a head and shoulders shot taken from a videotaped deposition I had given in the lawsuit filed by the Attorney General. The picture was grainy and it was obvious from my expression that I was not enjoying myself. The headline screeched something about administrators and the law. The article itself was a fair description of the issues involved in the charity care case in question; but that picture told its own story. It was so powerful and so negative that one of my friends, a prominent national healthcare CEO, actually asked me if I had been indicted.

If you are prominent, if you are successful, or if you are controversial you are going to have press—not just press about your institution, press about you! You can have good press or bad press. Good press is better. It's good for morale—your organization's and your own. Bad press is the opposite. When bad things are written about their leader, the team wonders about you; you wonder about yourself. The best policy is to try to keep press coverage focused on the organization, not on its leader. If you, as the leader, do receive press coverage, remember something I learned along the way: You are not as good as your good press; you are not as bad as your bad press. It helps not to believe either.

A chief executive must deal with the news media. It is part of the job. But, as you do, it is important to know something about the reporters with whom you will interact. First, they are a cynical bunch. All of their careers, they have been misled, lied to, and spun. They are prepared to believe the worst about everyone they come in contact with and their experience reinforces the belief—many people they cover have done something wrong or want to hide something. They may come with preconceived notions of what the story is going to be and have a hard time accepting facts that disagree with the preconception. They never know as much about your business as you do. They live off of controversy and conflict. If a story doesn't contain either, they often will try to manufacture them. Controversy and conflict sell their publications.

In dealing with reporters, always tell them the truth. You don't have to tell them everything you know, but what you do tell them must be true. If you lie to them, you have made an adversary for yourself and your institution. You do not want enemies who buy ink by the barrel and newsprint by the ton. Also, try to make their jobs easier. Give them written materials that contain facts and figures necessary for their stories. After an interview, always volunteer to be available to clarify any aspect of the interview. It is wise to ask the reporter to tape an interview and you should tape it as well. For the reporter, it is a much more accurate record of an interview than notes; for you, it can be useful later to have your exact words in full context if a dispute arises about the story. Finally, stay out of the gossip columns. A healthcare CEO is an important asset of the community engaged in serious work.

It doesn't help you or your institution to have you seen in your local newspaper as superficial.

Even though I worked my way through college as a newspaper reporter, I learned an important lesson about the press much later in life. I watched Ben Love dominate Texas banking for years as chairman and CEO of Texas Commerce Bankshares of Houston. He was respected and admired. For 17 straight years, he improved profits every quarter. The press loved him. Then, one quarter his banks' profits failed to exceed the previous quarter's. A front-page article in the Wall Street Journal took him apart. I learned there is no loyalty or love among the media. To the press, you are only as good as your most recent accomplishment. At any stumble, however insignificant or temporary, they are ready to pronounce your demise. They love to see the mighty fall.

When a CEO has assigned a COO responsibility for all of the organization, one of the two is unnecessary.

Res ipsa loquitur. The thing speaks for itself.

The dictatorial CEO limits the organization to his capabilities. All organizations, no matter how small, are larger than one individual.

We had a bright, up-and-coming young executive in our organization, named Gary Cottongim. He had done his residency training at Methodist and was selected to stay and fill an executive spot. He came to me with a problem. He had a proposal for an important personnel policy change and he wanted my advice on how to get it approved by the executive council, the group including all Methodist executives that was chaired by president Ted Bowen. I told him he needed to gain the support of all key executives before presenting it to the council. That would eliminate the possibility of public opposition. He took my advice, not only lining up the key executives in finance, human resources, and operations, but also gaining the support of *all* council members—except, of course, the president.

The council met Tuesday mornings at 10 o'clock. Gary's proposal was first on the agenda. He did a superb job of presenting it. When he was finished, Mr. Bowen looked at him and said: "You mean we have been doing this successfully around here for 20 years and now you come along, Cottongim, and want to change it?" Every head in the room swiveled toward Gary and every pair of eyes drilled into him as if to say, "Yeah, Cottongim." Mr. Bowen said, "Does anybody else think we should do this." Not a voice was raised in that room—not even mine. The proposal died right there.

Some organizations count the votes. In Mr. Bowen's, we weighed them. I know of no one more capable of carrying the whole burden of leading an organization than Ted Bowen, when he was in his prime. But, his authoritarian style limited the organization to his capabilities. Strong as they were, they were only the abilities of one man. No organization should be so limited.

The proposal was a good one. It should have passed.

You can make a Sumo sprint, but it is very difficult.

One of the most difficult tasks of my tenure as CEO was transforming a major teaching hospital—Methodist—from a fee-for-service-only institution to one capable of success in the world of managed care. The task took months and months and was resisted at almost every point by some element of each stakeholder group, including our affiliated medical school— Baylor. When it was over I was asked, "What was it like to bring Methodist into managed care?" I gave that considerable thought before I answered. Here is what I said: "It is like being asked to coach an entrant in the Olympic 100 meter dash—and to win. The good news is: Your entrant is a professional athlete. The bad news is: He is a Sumo wrestler."

We relied on a strong strategic planning process throughout my CEO years. Part of that process was an annual environmental assessment. In it, we took a careful look at both internal and external factors that would likely affect our business. From the mid-1980s to the early 1990s, the growth of managed care at the national, state, and local levels was a significant external factor we carefully monitored. We knew that eventually we would have to transition from fee-for-service to managed care; we didn't know when. But we did know it would not be easy.

As the teaching hospital component of an academic medical center, Methodist was ill-prepared for the transition. Its medical staff was almost entirely specialists or super specialists. They showed little interest in practicing HMO medicine—seeing the maximum number of patients in the minimum amount of time. Many were Baylor full-time faculty, who also had research and administrative duties that limited their practice time. There were only a handful of primary care physicians (managed-care gatekeepers) affiliated with Methodist. And, like most teaching hospitals, Methodist had a high cost structure.

For those reasons, and because we knew that the change was going to be gut-wrenching, we consciously planned to enter managed care as late as possible. We decided to wait until our physicians felt the pressure to see managed care patients, and then let them signal the hospital to transition. In the intervening years, we would maximize income from fee-for-service operations to build a substantial financial war chest. We believed we would need it.

In 1993, our physicians, who were steadily losing patients to managed care colleagues, began to bring pressure on management to open Methodist to managed care. It was time for a mission conference. Working for four months with the planning committee, augmented by additional physicians, we came to grips with the need to change our mission from being a fee-for-service, teaching hospital to becoming a managed care organization with a teaching hospital at its core. The new direction was approved in May 1994, beginning a time of tumultuous change for the organization—and for the Houston hospital market, which had been enjoying managed care price protection under Methodist's fee-for-service pricing umbrella.

With approval of the change of mission, I organized five task forces to effect the strategic and operating changes that would be necessary for us to be successful: cost, business development, integration, physicians, and medical school. An executive vice president and a prominent physician led each task force. Over the next 24 months, we implemented their work. Cost was the most wrenching. We had to bring expenses down to competitive levels. To make money on both managed care and Medicare, we reduced the workforce from more than 7,000 to fewer than 5,000 employees. This was particularly hard on me. As CEO, I had promised a no-layoff policy. We were not able to achieve that size staff reduction without layoffs. The only way I could cope with my decision to implement the reductions—including layoffs—was to tell myself that I was creating a stronger organization that would be more secure for the thousands of employees who remained. If neither IBM nor Japan could continue lifetime employment policies, how could Methodist sustain my no-layoff promise? We reduced annual expenses by an astounding $125 million.

As a fee-for-service-only hospital, Methodist of course had no managed care contracts. The business development task force took on that challenge. In the next two years, we signed 31 provider contracts and moved Houston's largest single block of HMO business—Prudential's—from Hermann Hospital to Methodist. The integration task force led us in the acquisition of our across-the-street neighbor, Diagnostic Hospital, and in the consolidation of Baytown's San Jacinto Methodist Hospital and the Visiting Nurses Association— Houston's largest home health agency—into our system. We began merger talks with St. Luke's Episcopal Hospital. The physician task force led us in the development of a primary care physician's organization, which was jointly owned by the doctors and the system. Finally, the medical school task force addressed the constant stream of issues our changed mission raised for medical education and the practices of the Baylor's faculty.

Those years of change were extraordinarily difficult for everyone. Our employees lost their sense of security. Physicians were upset, angry, and confused as their incomes dropped with the lower managed care rates and as the world of medicine they had known turned upside down. Board members, who were used to basking in praise for Methodist's management and patient care, now heard from physicians that management had "lost its vision" and that the cost reductions were harming patient care. The executive team leading the change was the same team that had believed in the former mission and was responsible for our past successes. For them, and for me, the effect of the change was visceral.

The experience of getting the Sumo to sprint is not one I will soon forget. It brought the whole question of the fate of the nation's venerable academic medical centers in the managed care environment into sharper focus for me.

The academic medical center is the combination of medical school, teaching hospital and clinics. It is historically bureaucratic, overly deliberative, and organizationally slow. It is a place of competition among full-time and voluntary faculty members, who vie with one another for academic prestige and for patients. Conflicts of interest and personal agendas abound. Authority is often diffuse. Department chairmen, at times, have more authority and influence than deans and presidents. A confusing array of departments, institutes, divisions, centers, and programs overlap in ways that defy logic and the organizational chart. It is anything but a nimble business unit. It was configured and developed for an earlier and simpler time of "soft" money and "seed" money, of cost-based reimbursement, of infinite federal and state dollars, and of incredible forbearance from the employers and insurers who paid the bills—in full and on time. It is, uniquely ill-suited to today's tough, competitive managed care environment.

Furthermore, the academic medical center is a bubbling stew of bench and clinical research, undergraduate and graduate medical and other professional education, and inpatient and outpatient clinical services and facilities. It has been a revered and successful institution—revered because of its many medical accomplishments and breakthroughs—and successful because, in the old fee-for-service market model, both referring physicians and discerning patients chose to use its extraordinary array of services. Plus, happily, someone else paid for those high-priced services. Today, the marketplace is clearly saying those days are over: "We, corporate America, will no longer pay a premium to such centers."

The reaction from the academic medical centers has been an agonizing mix of hand-wringing, indignation, disbelief, and various fits and starts at dealing with a new reality.

Questions about the future of such enterprises swirl through our medical schools, teaching hospitals, and the literature about them: "What is the national responsibility for graduate medical education? Who will pay for medical research? Should an all-payer fund be established to support physician training? How should such funds be raised—a general tax? Can teaching hospitals compete on a price basis? Can they survive at all?"

While I appreciate and, in fact, have lived the angst of such questions, I feel further disquiet as more troubling questions creep in: "Should medical education be subsidized at all? By anyone? Why should a privileged professional class, already in over supply, be granted an educational subsidy at public expense?"

I believe these questions will be answered in one of two frameworks. The first is the traditional one—I call it the "political, regulatory, Democrat, liberal, do-gooder" framework. Its premise is that academic medical centers are national treasures and that medical education and research are public responsibilities. Therefore, such institutions deserve regulatory and political protection. And, of course, subsidy.

The second framework I call the "market, competitive, Republican, conservative, mad dog" approach. Its premise is that such centers are leadership institutions and that they have the human and financial capital to lead in the marketplace. Medical education and research are just costs of doing business and, as at General Motors or IBM, they are routine manpower and R&D questions, to be dealt with in the normal course of business. And, of course, no subsidy.

I do not know which approach will ultimately prevail. It is possible that both might, as each state chooses its preferred framework in the face of federal inaction. In the meantime, here is some advice for leaders of academic medical centers. As someone who was there, I urge you to get on about the business of defining quality. A good start might be "patient-satisfying, price-competitive, appropriate health outcomes."

Once you've defined it, relentlessly work to:

- deliver higher patient satisfaction.
- devise new, less costly processes of care; and
- demonstrate superior, long-term medical outcomes.

The academic medical center is the home of the best and brightest minds in American medicine. If the possessors of that enormous intellect can stop mourning for the past and bemoaning the present, there is hope. To the extent that you can make the huge mental shift and develop the fortitude for change, we won't have to worry so much about graduate medical education and research—or the future of the academic medical center. If you can accomplish those things, governments and markets both will reward you.

It won't be easy. There are layers upon layers of history, ingrained culture, bureaucracy, and academic conceit. But you are the historic, as well as the current, preferred choice of both physicians and patients. You have the perception of quality. Now it is time to prove it.

It's time to make the Sumo sprint.

The CEO is like Caesar's wife.

In 62 B.C., Julius Caesar, not yet Consul of Rome but a rising public figure, discovered that his second wife, Pompeia, had intrigued with Claudius to violate the secret rites of Bona Dea, a fertility goddess worshipped only by Roman women. Saying, "Caesar's wife must be above suspicion," he divorced her.

Of course, he later became one of the most powerful and successful dictators in the history of ancient Rome—so powerful that his very name, Caesar, became synonymous with Consul. And, subsequent Roman rulers' wives were judged by the standard that Julius Caesar set when he divorced Pompeia: "Caesar's wife must be above suspicion."

It was not an easy task for the wife of the ruler of the most powerful nation in the world, living in its teeming capital city, to be "above suspicion." The Consul's wife was scrutinized wherever she appeared. Everything about her was observed, evaluated, and discussed. Her hair. Her jewelry. Her clothes. What she said (and to whom) and what she did (and with whom) were endless topics of gossip and speculation. Eventually, Caesar's wife was not only expected to be above suspicion, but beyond reproach.

Chief executives are like Caesar's wife. They are expected to be above suspicion and beyond reproach, and are the subject of constant observation, evaluation and discussion. Understanding this, and acting accordingly, can improve the prospects for the CEO's tenure and smooth relations with the board and management team.

Business expenses. Contract awards. Personal staff. Demeanor. These are, in my experience, areas of potential suspicion and reproach. Many CEO's in the healthcare industry have been disgraced and forced from their jobs because of mishandling their business expenses. Many have lost credibility because of favoritism in awarding construction, auditing, architectural, legal and other types of contracts. Some CEO's personal staff members act as if they are the imperial guard of an exalted potentate, treating callers and visitors to the corner office with disdain. And, some CEO's act as if they believe themselves entitled to some royal throne.

When I became a CEO, I addressed each of these potential minefields. I developed what I have since come to believe is a foolproof way of handling business expenses. Mine were sometimes very complicated, because I traveled and entertained not only on behalf of Methodist, but also for a number of associations—sometimes all simultaneously. I assigned our system's Internal Audit Department to prepare my monthly expense report including travel and entertainment expenses, plus any dues, fees, and subscriptions paid for me. Each report also included any personal expenses for which I would reimburse the organization—envelopes, stamps, and secretary's time for preparing personal letters, personal phone calls, photocopies, and the like. The report was then routed for approval to my chief financial officer, then to me, and, finally, to the chairman of the board. Each of us signed off on my monthly expenses. Internal Audit would then bill and collect expense reimbursements owed by other outside associations or organizations. It was my policy to personally pay for any item that caused a question at any point in the process. Annually, I insisted that the outside auditors review my business expenses and those of the executive team. With this system, I never had a problem with my expenses; and, since the process was one involving many layers in the organization, it was widely viewed as beyond suspicion.

Another pitfall for a CEO is the multiplicity of interested parties in the awarding of significant contracts. Having watched colleagues run afoul of board members pushing their contractor, banking, architect, and lawyer friends forward at contract time, I developed a system to protect the organization and me from improper influence. For a new contract, say a construction job, our facilities staff was instructed to send a request for proposal (RFP) to all qualified companies in Houston. The responses would be graded and ranked by the staff, then taken to a special committee made up of a senior executive, a member of the medical staff, and a board member. The committee would interview the top three or four firms and decide upon a recommendation to the full board of the system. The same process would work for continuing relationships—auditors, lawyers, bankers, and so forth. Every four or five years, RFPs would be sent to qualified firms, the staff would rate the responses, then either a standing or a special committee would interview the finalists and recommend the contract award to the board. As CEO, I oversaw the process, ensuring it was fair and beyond reproach, but I did not personally intervene. Therefore, I saved myself from a lot of sales calls from auditors and bankers who sought Methodist's business through its corner office and forestalled any potential unseemly influence from inside the organization. The process served the organization and me extremely well.

Staffs with imperial attitudes can seriously damage a CEO's reputation. And, sometimes he doesn't even know it's happening. The personal assistants of the CEO are a direct reflection of him and his style. The way they treat others is viewed by the organization as treatment by the CEO. I wanted to make sure that we set a tone of helpfulness, caring, and compassion in my office. First, I got the right people. Then I told them that the only unforgivable sins were arrogance, indifference, coldness, and rudeness to anyone who called, wrote, or entered our offices. June Dargahi, with her cheerful disposition and delightful British accent, managed the phones, the front door, and the first impression. Sue Wexler, my executive assistant for more than ten years, was my superb daily partner. David Huffstutler and Judy Gugenheim ran CEO staff services, preparing my speeches, doing staff analysis, and generally keeping me on track. The incomparable Pat Temple took care of VIP patients. All of them, my personal staff, *all of them* were the nicest, kindest, most patient people, not only to employees, executives, callers, visitors, or patients with problems, but to me.

Finally, a CEO's dress, comportment, demeanor, and manner of speaking and behaving, are all subjects of observation and comment inside and outside of his organization. I told myself from the very beginning that I was the leader of a great institution and that, as such, I owed it to the board, medical staff, volunteers, executives, and employees to always act with the dignity that organization deserved. I tried to dress conservatively and well; and to speak and conduct myself appropriately, without showing anger. While I certainly didn't do it perfectly, I always tried to improve.

When you move into the CEO office, it is a new ballgame. You are now the living symbol of what your organization is and what it wants to be. You are a public reflection of it. You are as scrutinized and as commented upon, as once was Caesar's wife. If you remember that, you will not only speak and act appropriately, you will install processes to insure that you remain above suspicion. And, beyond reproach.

When you have the money, you don't have the time.
When you have the time, you don't have the money.

When I became a CEO, I began a whirlwind of internal and external activities. Inside the healthcare system, my time was consumed with reorganization, strategic planning, establishing control and evaluation procedures, and directing the enterprise. I was building a culture and putting my personal stamp on the organization. Simultaneously, I stepped up my external activities, because I was learning that decisions made by associations, legislatures, state houses, congresses, the White House, and scattered and sundry bureaucrats had a direct, and often deleterious, effect on Methodist. Over the years I was chairman of the Texas Hospital Association, chairman of the National Taskforce on Healthcare Technology Assessment, a Prospective Payment Assessment commissioner, a board member of AAMC Council of Teaching Hospitals and the American Hospital Association. I spent time in the state capital and the nation's capital. I chaired the AHA and subsequently my professional society, the American College of Healthcare Executives.

The time flew by in a blur—like countryside seen from a fast-moving train through a rain-streaked window. I was very busy. I was busy, averaging more than 140 nights a year out of Houston. I was constantly overbooked. PROPAC meetings conflicted with AHA meetings, which were scheduled on the dates my various boards were to meet. Invariably, I would have to leave one meeting before it was over in order to arrive at another—late. It was a constant juggling act. I was a good juggler, but periodically an Indian club clanked to the floor.

And, there was no time to enjoy the spectacular ride. On the road, meetings were held at some of the best hotels and resorts in the United States—lovely places in Florida, Hawaii, Arizona. There were beaches and championship golf courses. Often, my colleagues would bring their spouses and stay extra days in those lovely settings. My rushed schedule usually brought me in late on the night before the meeting. It was room-service dinner, up early to speak or chair a meeting, and then catch a cab back to the airport—either to rush home or speed on to the next meeting. If I were lucky, I might get to walk around the pool or out along the beach for a few minutes before catching the cab. When I returned home, all the accumulated correspondence and issues had to be handled. Almost every weekend was spent catching up on reams of paperwork and stacks of professional reading. Time. Time. Time. There weren't enough minutes in the hour, hours in the day, days in the month, months in the year.

How much did those five-star hotels and those posh resorts cost? I had no idea. I rarely glanced at the daily rates. The stays were someone else's concern. They were paid for on various expense accounts, not by me. All those beautiful places paid for by someone else and no time to even enjoy them for the scheduled length of the meeting, much less time to stop and smell the bougainvillea.

Two powerful things happen when you leave an executive position for good. One, you are gifted with extra time. Two, the big salary and bonuses vanish, along with the expense-paid trips to five-star land. (But, I have since had the opportunity to go to several at my own expense. Do you have any idea what those places cost? It's outrageous!)

I've always tried to live my life and conduct myself professionally so that I wouldn't have to say "I should have done things differently." But, I do sometimes wistfully think of those beautiful places seen through that rain-streaked window from that speeding train. More time when money was not a problem would have been nice; more money now that I have extra time couldn't hurt. Could it?

A CEO's success or failure is only evident years after he's gone.

An effective chief executive should be focused on those things only he can do for his organization—strategy, policy, external relations, and the management of change. Planning (or in other words, the formulation of strategy), is the first task of management. As such, it is the CEO's first responsibility. The development of policies to guide the organization, the management of important external relationships, and the orchestration of change are likewise uniquely the province of the chief executive. They all have one thing in common: They impact the organization over the long term.

In evaluating a CEO's success or failure, it is of little consequence that he was popular with the board, physicians, or employees. It is of like consequence that his programs were successful while he was present to oversee them. The crucial test of the chief executive's success or failure is this: Did he leave the organization with the right strategic and financial resources to meet the future?

I have watched a number of system chiefs enjoy enormous success and accolades during their tenures, only to see years later that their strategies and policies did not meet the test of time. I have concluded that it requires at least ten years after the departure of a CEO to reach reliable conclusions about the effect of that person's leadership on the organization.

The lesson here to a sitting CEO is twofold. First, focus your energies and activities on those things that only the chief can effectively do. Second, make your decisions based upon your best judgment of the long-term positive impact on the organization.

Planning

Crisis management is no management at all.

In the healthcare industry we see abundant crises. Nurse shortages, budget overruns, investigative reports, government inspections, lawsuits, and bad publicity are a few of the regulars. All of them must be handled by an organization's leadership team. But, if rushing from crisis to crisis is all the executives do, the organization is not being led.

The problem with crisis management is that it crowds out the time, energy, and resources for long-term, strategic management. And, it can become habit-forming. Putting out organizational fires is a legitimate executive task. But fire-fighting must be planned for and managed, just like any other corporate challenge.

The first priority for your management team is to have a strategic plan that is well understood and well communicated. It should be the product of a dynamic planning process that includes the leaders of all relevant stakeholder groups. And, it should be tested against the internal and external environment on an annual basis and modified appropriately. Once modified, it should form the basis for the year's operating and capital budgets as well as management's annual goals and objectives. Executive compensation should be based upon the accomplishment of those strategic tasks. Without this basic road map to the future, including executive incentives to follow it, your organization is adrift.

Even a sound strategic plan can be short-circuited by the need to stamp out organizational brush fires. Your job as leader is to insure that doesn't happen. The strategic plan's objectives must be met and the fires must be extinguished, as well. Do not allow the noise and heat to throw your organization into chaos. You will do that if you pull people from their continuing leadership responsibilities and assign them full-time to handle the crisis. When the fire alarm sounds, you must be calm and organized. Assign a line executive the crisis management responsibility or, alternatively, create a crisis management task force. In either case, make available the necessary staff and financial resources to deal with the situation. But, through your leadership and your communications, emphasize the organization's strategic and long-range tasks. Don't give in to the temptation to hurl yourself at the problem and work exclusively on it.

Organizations need leaders who understand that crises are a routine part of corporate life. Executives are expected to deal with them—in a calm and well-organized manner. But, more importantly, leaders are expected to keep the organization focused on the future, even when the brush fires are flaring.

Short-term management is no management at all.

The charter issued by the state of Texas says that The Methodist Hospital in Houston "will provide hospital services to the sick and injured, in perpetuity." In perpetuity! It does not say that it will do so in good times only. Or that there are exceptions for hyperinflation, depression, over-regulation, or brutal competition. The intent is quite clear. Favored by the state as a tax-exempt organization, Methodist was expected to provide those vital services and keep on providing them.

Our executive team took that charter literally to heart. We knew that hospitals were a special management challenge. They were capital intensive, requiring sophisticated buildings and expensive, highly technical equipment. They were also labor intensive, with salaries and benefits accounting for about 60 percent of operating costs. We were aware that many similarly chartered U.S. hospitals were literally hand-to-mouth operations, with meager financial reserves and thin margins. And we knew that momentous changes and pressures would inevitably arise for the healthcare industry in the future, and that those changes would impact our institution. We didn't know specifically what those changes and pressures would be, but we knew they would come.

Keeping all this in mind, we assessed Methodist's future building needs, including replacement of all existing facilities, and estimated the financial reserves necessary to see the organization through the rough times ahead. That assessment was quite an eye-opener. To operate Methodist in perpetuity was going to require a lot of money!

The team developed and implemented a long-term plan to secure the institution's financial security. Every Methodist system corporation was accountable for a positive operating margin—usually about five percent above the inflation rate. We used tax-exempt financing as a cash management tool, borrowing at low interest rates to finance needed buildings and equipment, while placing our excess operating income in higher earning investments. As we accumulated reserves, we employed professional investment advisors to manage the funds for us. As a result of a continuous flow of operating earnings into investments and sound portfolio returns, we amassed nearly $2 billion in investments by the time I left the organization.

The fact that Methodist made and accumulated that kind of money attracted a lot of attention, some of it very critical. It was hard for me to understand those who thought it somehow wrong for a hospital to be financially secure. I could look across Main Street from our campus and see Rice University. That distinguished, non-profit institution—much less capital- and labor-intensive than Methodist—had an endowment larger than $2 billion and no one carped about that. In spite of the criticism, we took the long view, and continued to accumulate the funds necessary for an uncertain future. Subsequent changes in the industry—managed care proliferation and Medicare cutbacks among them—have proved the wisdom of our long-term approach.

I believe that executives of non-profit hospitals have a sacred obligation to provide care to the community's sick and injured people as long as that care is needed. To do that you need financial security. If you are losing money on current operations and you are not accumulating reserves, you are jeopardizing the future of your institution. If you are managing for the short term—this year, next quarter, next week—you are not securing your organization's future. And if this is the case, you are not managing at all.

Take a new look. Call the team together and peer hard into the future. Develop a realistic assessment of the hospital's financial needs for the long haul and start working to find the funds to meet those needs. Your institution is expected to be healing the sick and injured for a long time. "In perpetuity" means forever.

The plan is important,
but the planning process is paramount.

Planning is the very first task of management. Without a plan, leaders can't know where to take their organizations. But, while having a plan is very important, it is the process of planning that makes the difference between success or failure.

Properly done, a strategic planning process brings to the table leaders of each important group that has a stake in the future of the organization. In Methodist's case, the strategic planning committee consisted of the senior executives, board members, officers of the medical staff, and leaders of our affiliated medical school. We met frequently to evaluate our progress and make course corrections as the industry winds blew against us. The give and take in those meetings brought consensus. More importantly, they brought commitment. Stakeholders who have committed to a strategic direction increase the odds of success. Uncommitted stakeholders insure failure.

As an offshoot of the planning process, I created a policy council which met every Tuesday. Around the breakfast table, we shared information and coordinated major decisions. The group included the chairman of the Methodist System's board and its two vice chairmen, the officers of the medical staff, the dean of Baylor College of Medicine, my three System executive vice presidents, and me. I had gotten agreement from the medical school officials and our medical staff leaders that neither group would take actions affecting Methodist without first bringing it to the policy council. Important recommendations to the Baylor board by the school's executive staff and recommendations by the medical staff officers to their executive committee would be reviewed by the policy group, if they had ramifications for Methodist. In return, I committed to them that my executive team and I would not take any major financial, operating, or strategic recommendation to Methodist's board without first discussing it in the council.

The process worked extremely well. It coordinated our decision-making and prevented official actions by any group from surprising or embarrassing the others. Often, proposed actions were discussed and modified by the policy council. Sometimes they were shortstopped completely. But, the most important aspect of the policy process was the fact that every Tuesday morning the leaders of Methodist came face to face to discuss strategy and coordinate decision-making for the good of the organization.

If you are an executive in a corporation that has many stakeholder groups—such as a hospital or a health system—it is vital to your success as a leader to develop processes to coordinate and lead them. Strategic planning is a function that demands such processes. Properly managed, the face-to-face interchange among the stakeholder leaders in the planning process facilitates communication, builds consensus, and brings commitment. There is nothing inherent in any plan that does that.

Strategy

Those who pursue excellence probably will survive.
Those who pursue survival probably will not.

At the beginning of the Twentieth-first Century, the healthcare industry in the United States is in considerable disarray. Its principal components—doctors, hospitals, and insurers—have lost their historic sense of place in the healthcare system and have invaded each other's territory. Doctors are owning and operating hospitals and outpatient treatment facilities; hospitals are buying physician practices and operating HMOs; and insurers dabble in both hospital and physician practice ownership. Physicians are demoralized, confused, and angry. Their incomes fall as managed care and Medicare reduce payments to them. A substantial percentage of them would not enter the field of medicine, if they had it to do over again, and would not advise their children to be physicians. Hospitals face daily pressure from declining revenues at the same time the service and care expectations of their patients rise. And, the HMOs bleed cash. It is not an attractive picture.

If you are a healthcare executive, I have just described your working environment. It is the environment to which you have entrusted your career. It is not likely to change significantly for the remainder of your professional life and, sadly, there is not much you and your fellow executives can do to alter that environment. You have two options. One, you can hang your head, get depressed, bemoan the situation, get angry, and just shuffle along. Two, you can raise your chin, get pumped up, accept the situation, get busy, and shoot for excellence. The first is a prescription for failure. If that's the attitude you bring to the leadership of your organization, your organization will probably fail. If that's your personal and professional attitude, you and your career will probably fail. But, if you take the second attitude, you have a good chance to survive this miserable time in our industry.

You can't do anything about the times. You can do everything about you. Adjust that attitude, gear up for excellence. There are no guarantees that you will achieve true excellence; there are no guarantees that your organization or your own career will survive even if you do. But, if you strive for excellence, you improve the chances for survival and success. And, if you fail, you will have the comfort of knowing that you failed while trying to do something extraordinary. Go for excellence—organizational excellence, leadership excellence, professional excellence, and personal excellence. Go for excellence, because you only have one career. You only have one life.

Outstanding service is
the most effective marketing strategy.

At an executive council meeting early in my tenure as a chief executive officer, a junior executive was reporting on his departments' efforts to implement the recommendations of the Caring Through Service task force. The group had been established to overhaul the service experience of The Methodist Hospital, whose mission, after all, was "to provide the best care and service anywhere." In his report, he said, "Mr. Mathis has us all nervous, nervous, nervous about service, service, service."

And, he was right. If there was anything I passionately believed in, it was our service mission. The hospital's medical and nursing care were superb, but I knew that our patients did not have a way of judging them. They couldn't tell if the physicians reading their x-rays were the best at what they did; they had no way of knowing if the MRI scans were of the highest quality. But, what they could judge was service. That's what all Americans can judge. With more than 60 percent of us working in service jobs, and all of us experiencing service of one kind or another every day, we are experts on it.

We sure gave service a go at Methodist. I made it a top CEO priority. At every all-employee meeting, I emphasized our service mission, explaining how each encounter between an employee and a patient was a "moment of truth" for the organization. We developed service-training courses and put all employees—including executives—through them. We learned along the way that better service requires management, training, and constant communication. Better service also changed our facilities. We developed a front-of-the-house/back-of-the-house approach. The front of the house—the part patients and visitors saw—was beautifully decorated; the back of the house, where employees had their workspaces, was more utilitarian. We created the patient center. It was on the first floor of our principal building, next to the main entrance. Patients who needed something from the hospital—anything at all—would go to the center and be greeted by a concierge who would arrange to have their request met. They then enjoyed refreshments in the beautifully appointed center, while employees from various departments tracked down and delivered the requested item: a copy of a medical record, a pharmacy prescription, a copy of the hospital bill, etc. No longer did our patients have to chase all over our many buildings to transact their business with us. The patient center made it a one-stop operation.

Even the main entrance was redesigned with a long, covered arrival drive staffed by doormen, bellmen, and valet parkers. Upon entering the building, patients saw a sparkling fountain in a sun-lit atrium. No frightening hospital sights and smells were in evidence.

And, we changed our systems of service, reengineering them to be more patient friendly. The results were startling. Letters and calls of complaint were replaced by raves about our service. And, business boomed: Patient encounters rose year after year.

Which brings me to marketing strategy. I have rarely seen hospital print or television advertising that I thought was effective. So much of it has been of the "We-are-St. Somewhere-and-We-Care" type. I believe that the best marketing strategy is to delight patients, exceed their expectations.   And, the best advertising component of marketing is to discharge highly pleased patients every day to their communities to sing the praises of the service they experienced in your hospital.

You can begin to do this by rethinking everything about the hospital—facilities, systems, and training—from the patient's point of view. Make it the boss' priority. Make sure everyone involved in the organization is nervous, nervous, nervous about service, service, service.

When the lion lies down with the lamb,
there is no fear in the heart of the lion.

In a utopian world—a landscape of peace and love—the lion will lie down with the lamb. Have you ever wondered what that lion might be thinking; what that lamb might be thinking? I have. The lamb must be pretty edgy. With no natural defenses against predators, lambs have, for all of the history of the world, been meals for powerful and hungry lions. To the lamb, this new world of peace and love is great in concept, but if it doesn't work out, lying next to a lion is not any place to be. The lion? He doesn't give it a thought.

This is a parable about power.

The Methodist Hospital and St. Luke's Episcopal Hospital sit side by side in Houston's world-famous Texas Medical Center. Connected by tunnels, the two institutions have an overlapping medical staff, boast strong competing cardiovascular surgery programs, and have in the past shared purchasing, laundry, and maintenance services. Both are non-profit, protestant religious organizations. Competing in a regional market where hospitals have an average occupancy of 45 percent, Methodist and St. Luke's were excellent candidates for a merger. Twice, we tried. Twice, we failed.

On the second attempt, we nearly succeeded. St. Luke's insisted on a merger of equals, while Methodist sought a proportionate combination. When the investment bankers rendered their asset valuations of the two organizations, all of St. Luke's assets, including its office building and its foundation, did not equal Methodist Hospital's assets alone (the Methodist Healthcare System also included other hospitals, numerous office buildings, and a $1 billion plus foundation, in addition to Methodist Hospital). The asset valuation only solidified our respective positions; Methodist couldn't agree to a merger of equals and St. Luke's wouldn't lie down with the lion.

Often, as an executive, you will find yourself in a disproportionate power relationship. If you are the party with less power, you build personal or organizational safeguards to protect yourself or your institution. That's what St. Luke's was doing. If you are the one with more power, you have a more complex burden. You, the lion, really don't need to give the imbalance of power much thought, unless, of course, it is important for you to have the lamb lie comfortably beside you. If that is the case, it is incumbent upon you to calm the lamb's fears and to help structure the safeguards that will make that possible.

There are lions and lambs, side by side, in marriages, in the executive suite, in business, and in mergers. If they are to peacefully co-exist, it is the lions who must mind their manners.

The consequences of inaction are generally worse than the consequences of action.

Studies have shown that most unsuccessful Fortune 500 CEOs fail not because of poor planning, but because of poor execution. And, it is execution that counts in corporate leadership. All of the beautifully conceived strategic plans, objectives, and tactics are nothing, if the leadership team members don't roll up their sleeves and just do it.

At Methodist, strategic planning was the responsibility of the key operations executives and the CEO. I organized it that way because I knew that after the planning was done, it would take commitment and hard work to make the plan become reality. The operations people were the ones who would have to make it happen. Since they led the planning process, their commitment was built in. It was their plan; their reputations—and their compensation—were on the line. So, when the team committed to strategic objectives, you could bet your shirt that they would be accomplished.

If you are one of those executives whose business unit is losing money and is mired in indecision, your problem is execution. Perhaps you are unsure of what to do in a difficult environment. You are afraid of the consequences of action. If this is happening to you and your organization, snap out of it. In the army, they told us young combat-bound officers, "do something, even if it's wrong." That's good advice. There is energy in action. Diligently executed, any one of a number of different strategies will succeed. Of course, you want to try to do the right thing—select the strategy that has the best chance of success. But, if you and your team are action-oriented, even a bad strategy can be successful.

Pull yourself out of your indecisiveness. If you don't, the spirit of your people will die. And your organization may, too. Act. Act to cut expenses. Act to restore profitability. Act to reenergize your organization.

And, if you fail? You failed charging ahead with your sword in your hand, leading your troops, instead of cowering in your tent behind the lines.

Yesterday's wisdom is today's folly;
today's wisdom is tomorrow's folly.

Yesterday's wisdom: The Hill-Burton act. The idea was that every community across American should have its own hospital. Federal money was made available in grants to accomplish that purpose. During the sixties and seventies, hundreds of hospitals were constructed in small and medium-sized towns throughout the states. The result: Hundreds of under-occupied, struggling hospitals. Today's folly.

Yesterday's wisdom: diversification. The idea was that hospitals should expand beyond their core missions of patient care and service to add profitable business lines. During the late seventies and the eighties, hospitals went into businesses they knew little about—construction, catering, restaurants, and even cattle ranching, in one high-profile case. The result: Hundreds of failed businesses and millions of dollars diverted from patient care—wasted. Today's folly.

Yesterday's wisdom: Hospitals should purchase physician practices. The idea was that hospitals could gain control of their distribution systems—by owning the physicians' practices, they control the physicians. In the nineties, hospitals and systems were paying and overpaying hundreds of thousands of dollars to effect such control. The result: Once-profitable physician practices lost money while newly rich physicians retired in their offices. Today's folly.

The healthcare industry has been led by followers. I call it the *Modern Healthcare* syndrome. If it's on that cover, it must be the thing to do! Our industry leaders rush from one new idea to the next in search of the answer—the silver bullet solution to their strategic, financial, and operational problems. THERE IS NO SILVER BULLET.

Today's wisdom: Hospitals should own HMOs. The idea is that the HMOs control the flow of dollars in the healthcare system; therefore, hospitals need to own them to rise from the bottom of the industry's food chain. From the 70s through the 90s, hospital systems—both for-profit and not-for-profit—proved over and over again that hospitals and HMOs are incompatible businesses. The result: After losing millions and millions of dollars, hospitals are abandoning or selling their HMOs and returning to their core competencies. Tomorrow's folly.

And, today's greatest wisdom: Modifying the health-care system will control healthcare spending. The idea is that tinkering with the system—managed care, regulation, technology, etc.—will ultimately be successful in reining in healthcare spending. How wrong that is. It ignores powerful forces: the growth and aging of our people and their wealth and expectations. Where long-term costs are concerned, the healthcare system in America is its own worst enemy. It has found cures for the infectious diseases that used to kill children and young adults by the millions, then began a series of breakthroughs in heart disease and cancer treatment. The lives spared go on and on. From the perspective of cost to the system, it was cheaper when people died young.

Add to this fact a growing and aging population with wealth and high expectations and you have the prescription for huge additional expenditures for healthcare. The baby boomers are about to inherit ten trillion dollars from their parents and grandparents and, if necessary, these narcissistic sons and daughters will spend every cent to extend life and improve its quality. They intend to look good on the tennis courts in their eighties. And, when they seek care and service from the system, they will want it on their terms, with a smile, and make it snappy. The idea that somehow managed care or some other artful tweaking of the system will stem that tide is laughable. Tomorrow's folly.

If you are in the arena today, know that the battle hasn't even begun. If you think you have seen change in your career, it is nothing compared with what is coming. To cope with that change and be successful, you will need all the skill, intelligence, judgment, hard work, and luck you can muster. The answers won't be easy to find but you'll be wise to look close to home. The adage that all healthcare is local is true. Solutions must be found that uniquely fit each institution and each community. Be skeptical of the accepted wisdom. If everyone knows it is the right thing to do, it probably isn't.

And, as much as you and I love to read about who is in, who is out, and what is new, don't get your business strategy from the latest edition of *Modern Healthcare*.

Physician

Physician executive: an oxymoron

It is not impossible, but it is very difficult for a physician—absent specific leadership training—to be an effective executive. Consider what it takes to become a successful physician. In high school, prospective medical students are challenged to be outstanding individual performers. They are expected to excel academically. The pressure pattern continues into the college years, where the physicians-to-be must exceed the intellectual attainments of other prospective professionals. Medical school and post-graduate training experiences focus on the ability of the individual to diagnose and to treat—a solo responsibility. All of physicians' education and training is concentrated to produce outstanding individual performers: self-sufficient, self-reliant, self-confident medical practitioners.

What about executives? They are leaders, persuaders, team builders, communicators, organizers, people who are expected to get the best out of other individual performers. But, mostly, executives are leaders. Leadership is not an individual act. It is interaction. It is a participatory process, bringing people together to combine their best collective efforts to accomplish organizational goals. Successful executives reach out, share information, empower others to act, and creates an environment of participation and excitement about the possibilities of group achievement.

I have seen hospital boards choose physicians as chief executives who have no prior executive or leadership training.

In many cases the institution is troubled. In all cases, the industry environment is troubled. The search process parades in front of the board a series of professional executives who in interviews do not minimize the potential difficulties that they foresee or maximize the chances of success for the organization. An influential board member, in desperation, turns to a physician on the staff. The physician is clear-eyed and confident. "I'll tell you what needs to be done around here." He is interviewed by other board members who are swept away by his self-confidence and his assurances of successful change. "We have found the savior."

The physician is hired. His first official act as CEO is to decimate the management team (obviously, the reason for the organization's trouble) and begins to take on the organization's problems— all of them—personally. If a matter comes to his attention, it is his problem to solve.

The outcome—the deleterious effects of solo "leadership"—usually takes a year or two. Sometimes the CEO's colleagues on the medical staff turn against him. Sometimes the organizational chaos is so dispiriting that a change must be made. Sometimes the physician CEO is simply overwhelmed by the magnitude and the multitude of the problems and decisions he has taken on personally. The end result: a failed physician executive and a still troubled healthcare institution.

I don't mean to disparage physicians. Throughout my career, I have been a great admirer of doctors as clinicians and as individuals. But, I think I have developed a realistic view of physicians. All of that success in high school and in college, all of the pressures and sleepless nights of medical school, all the grueling years of residency and fellowship training can produce great physicians and surgeons. But, nothing in all of that success guarantees the physician can become a successful businessman, a successful real estate baron, a successful oil magnate. Or, a successful executive.

Physician businessman: another oxymoron.

It was a genuine pleasure to listen to him. He had always had an interest in the food business and he had created a new concept for a restaurant. As we sat comfortably in my second floor office drinking coffee, he told me how he was going to insure quality in his new fast-food business and what he expected the demand to be. He knew the break-even point and expected his new venture would be profitable within one year of opening. He even had created a delightful jingle to advertise the product. He had come to see me as a courtesy to tell me that he was renting space for his new restaurant in one of Methodist's physician office buildings—a prime location with huge pedestrian exposure. He wasn't your typical entrepreneur—he was a physician, one of the leading specialists on the hospital's medical staff. When I asked him where he was going to get the initial and working capital for his venture, he replied "physician friends."

Within nine months of opening, the new business was bankrupt. The physician entrepreneur had lost his entire stake in it and so had the friends who had invested as much as $15,000 each. Here was another sad example of a physician straying from the business he knows—providing medical treatment—to lose his shirt on a business he doesn't know.

I respect and admire physicians. Throughout my career, I have watched as physicians and surgeons have worked incredibly long hours, from dusk to dawn to dusk, to save the life of a patient. They can be wonderfully caring people. More than one has sat at my bedside for hours when I was in a medical crisis. They are among the very top of the economic and social elite in the United States. They are consummate professionals, the best and brightest of the best and brightest. But, when they leave the confines of medicine, they can be a danger to themselves and to others.

Oil well drilling partnerships. Real estate deals. Office building joint ventures. Cattle feed lot operations. Through the years, I have seen physicians pour their hard-earned money into these and worse investments, never to see it again. Incredibly wealthy, sophisticated, world-famous Dr. Denton Cooley went bankrupt in the real estate business in Texas. And, he was someone who billed nearly $10 million dollars a year for work with his hands! Why do they do it?

I suspect that physicians have been so much smarter than everyone else for so much of their lives—high school and college particularly reinforces this—that they begin to believe intellectual prowess makes them omnipotent. They assume that their mastery of medicine is transferable to other fields of endeavor. Perhaps many also, like too many of their less sophisticated fellow human beings, believe that it is possible to "get rich quick."

To the young doctor just starting out, I would urge you to be an outstanding businessman! An outstanding businessman in the only business you know—medicine. If you are in solo practice or in a group practice, manage your staff, accounts receivables and payables, your marketing, and your finances. Make it the best small business it can be. As for your personal investments, leave the glitz and glitter alone. Forget the possibility of getting rich quickly. Forget the limited partnerships and special joint ventures. Fully fund your 401K and put your extra money in conservative investments—a mix of certificates of deposit, municipal bonds, growth mutual funds, and quality large company stocks. Hire a professional investment or trust advisor to look after your funds. Stay away from purebred horses and cattle. Don't buy airplanes or yachts—rent them, if you must. In the end, you will be much better off financially and you will have spared yourself and your family the sickening investment roller coaster plunges that your older, and hopefully now wiser, colleagues have endured.

And, if a colleague approaches you to invest in a fast-food venture, just say "no."

There is a lesson here for the healthcare executive, as well. Increasingly, you will be in business with physicians. Hospitals owning physician practices and diagnostic and therapeutic joint ventures between hospitals and doctors are two examples. When you go into business with them, remember this maxim. Let the physicians practice medicine. You provide the business plan, the leadership and the financial and operating acumen.

*Talk to one physician and
you have talked to one physician.*

I spent my entire career interacting with physicians and I am still baffled that they have so much trouble with the basics of organizations. They don't get delegation; they don't understand process; and they don't believe in being represented by others. Some examples:

The president of Methodist's medical staff had an issue that needed resolution by the organization's executive committee. He handpicked doctors to form a task force to study the issue and make recommendations to the committee. He, himself, served on the task force. But when it made a recommendation with which he did not personally agree, he led his other two medical staff officers in opposing his own task force's work when it was presented to the executive committee. The recommendation failed to pass.

Several groups of hospital-based specialists decided to merge into a large, regional group. They elected a board and asked me to advise them about board operations. "Since we are the board, aren't we in charge? Don't we have the power to make decisions?" I told them that, of course, the board had the power to act and could make decisions, but that their organization was not like a regular corporation. It would be making decisions about their partners' personal money, not a corporation's income statement. They must be very careful and take time to build consensus among their partners before acting. However, the board members were full of their authority and they proceeded to exercise their power in a way that they perceived to be their right as board members. The group disintegrated.

On any number of occasions, when I was speaking with a physician about the official position taken by the medical staff executive committee on a given issue, I was told, "Well, they don't speak for me." This scenario was repeated with a wide variety of physicians.

It was sometimes maddening. We would put together a group of doctors to tackle some issue and work hard to gain consensus. When the work was done, other physicians would say, "They don't speak for me." Even when the organized medical staff selected the members for a task force to address a problem, if a physician didn't like the outcome, it was, "They don't speak for me."

I learned that when you had the views of one physician, that's what you had—the views of one physician. Consensus-building was a challenge even in the relatively easy zone of physician-management interaction—the hospital's medical staff organization. When it came to business operations involving their practices and their money, no one could represent them, they wouldn't delegate authority, and they wanted an equal voice in decision-making.

Partly because of these physician peculiarities, I refused to have a position of Vice President for Medical Affairs in my organization. Such positions, usually filled by physicians, are created to handle medical staff relationships. I refused for two reasons. First, I believed that medical staff relations were my job and that of our operating executives. Second, I believed that the medical staff would view a physician who became a vice president as a member of management, not as a colleague.

The lesson in all this is one that every successful healthcare executive has learned. Working in organizations with physicians takes extraordinary patience. It takes intense communication, both at the group and the individual levels. It takes extra efforts to build consensus. And it takes unusual organizational structures to incorporate them into decision-making. Physicians are the heart and soul of the healthcare industry in this country, God love them, but they are not easy to work with. But, work with them you must. If you are in healthcare, they are the business. If you don't believe it, just ask one of them. Then another. Then another. Then another. Good luck.

Government

It is dangerous to fight government...
and difficult to win.

The Hermann Hospital scandal rocked the Houston establishment. The Texas Medical Center institution was established under the last will and testament of George Hermann, an eccentric Swiss immigrant businessman who left his entire fortune—a considerable one—for the establishment of a hospital for Houston's poor. Trustees of the estate were to be chosen from among the city's leading citizens. By the time the state's attorney general, investigative reporters for local Channel 13 and the *Houston Post* and *Chronicle*, and the local district attorney finished digging through the scandal's muck, members of the hospital's management team and some of those leading citizen-trustees were indicted. Charges ranged widely over a venal landscape: embezzlement, misappropriation of hospital assets, inappropriate expenditures, lavish perquisites, and outright theft. The institution itself was charged with failure to provide sufficient charity healthcare to meet the intent of Mr. Hermann's will. At the scandal's end, prominent Houstonians were convicted of felonies and several, including Hermann's chief executive officer, were in the penitentiary. It was not one of Houston's prettier moments.

Houston's largest private, not-for-profit, teaching hospital—The Methodist Hospital—sits immediately across the street from Hermann. As investigative reporters and newscasters won awards and as district attorneys and attorney general staffers won promotions for their roles in exposing and prosecuting the Hermann misdeeds, others began to explore

THE MATHIS MAXIMS

that same path to awards and success. If Hermann was that bad, other hospitals must be rife with corruption. A little more than two years into my tenure as CEO at Methodist, a local television reporter, began a week-long series of investigative reports on "fiscally robust" Methodist Hospital. That report began a battle with the press and the state of Texas that continued for nine years. It was a fight I did not choose. Its early skirmishes made me grow up quickly as a CEO. Before the war was over, Methodist had been investigated repeatedly by the press, the attorney general's office, the Texas Department of Health, audited by the IRS, and had been featured in the crossfire of television's internecine warfare. I had been deposed by the AG, been through a hearing by U.S. Congressional Investigations committee, matched barbs with Sam Donaldson on *Prime Time Live* and had been the subject of an attack video produced by the office of the Attorney General of Texas. This saga eventually had a positive outcome. And, there were many lessons learned; not the least of which was: It is dangerous to fight government...and difficult to win.

Here is the saga.

November 4, Year 1

A local investigative reporter blares over the 6 o'clock news on Channel 11 that he is beginning an expose on the "financially successful" Methodist Hospital. After reviewing the Hermann scandal, he implies that Methodist is just as bad. He alleges Methodist has violated its nonprofit charter, has inappropriate expenditures, has provided inadequate charity care, and has, like Hermann, Board members who have conflicts of interest. The series runs four days and ends with the reporter saying that Methodist's former employees are "coming forward" and that this story is just beginning.

November 5, Year 1

A *Houston Post* reporter, fresh from a series of critical articles on the Harris County Hospital District (Methodist's neighbor in the Texas Medical Center), requests "in writing" Methodist's financial records. He reiterates the Channel 11 allegations and drops a nuclear warhead: He has contacted the office of the Texas Attorney General, and an assistant AG alludes to an "investigation" of Methodist.

November 8, Year 1

The *Houston Chronicle's* distinguished medical writer requests "in writing" Methodist's financial records. On advice of legal counsel, Methodist refuses to comply with the request arguing in our response that such records contain proprietary and competitive information. Further, we respond that Methodist is exempt from such public disclosure under the Texas Non-Profit Corporation Act.

November 13, Year 1

The *Post's* reporter presents his second written request for records. He copies the office of the Harris County District Attorney and asks for a ruling from the DA, a hard-nosed, no-nonsense Texas law man.

November 15, Year 1

Investigative reporters. Television commentaries. Assistant attorneys general talking "investigation." The District Attorney. An incredible series of sickening body blows. The management team and I are literally in shock. We have done nothing wrong. What is happening to this great and internationally renowned hospital? We engage the crisis-management public relations firm, Burson-Marsteller—the people who handled the Tylenol poisoning scare. With their help, we begin the development of a comprehensive public statement, one that we hope will answer every single allegation and innuendo that has been raised over the past eleven gut-wrenching days.

November 25, Year 1

The Chairman of the Board, A. Frank Smith, Jr., and I meet with Attorney General Jim Mattox. We have requested the meeting. We tell him we have nothing to hide and volunteer to permit the AG's staff to review all of our financial records. The Attorney General is a life-long Dallasite, a former U.S. Democratic Congressman from that area. He is known to be one of the most tenacious and confrontational of politicians in a state known for tenacious and confrontational office holders. He tells us we are *not* under investigation, but "why don't we just agree to an 'informal' investigation?" Chills!

November 26, Year 1

Methodist releases its public statement to the Houston media. It refutes every assertion. It states, "On our own initiative, Methodist met with the Attorney General to discuss allegations. A mutual decision was reached to allow an informal investigation." Incredibly, the same day, the Attorney General announces a "probe" of Methodist's charity care and finances. So much for our "mutual decision."

December 12, Year 1

The Assistant AG and two assistants tour Methodist Hospital and review financial records.

December 25, Year 1

Not the happiest Christmas in memory in the homes of Methodist Hospital employees, physicians, volunteers, and board members. It is worst in the home of the Chief Executive Officer.

January 3, Year 2

The Harris County District Attorney finally speaks to the question posed to him by the *Post* reporter on November 13: Does the law require Methodist to make its financial records available to the public? The answer? The DA punts. He formally requests a ruling from the Texas Attorney General's office on the records issue specifically asking: "Must Methodist release its financial records to the media? Is Methodist exempt from such disclosure because it is a denominational organization under the law?"

January 8-9, Year 2

The Assistant AG and his assistants return to the hospital and review additional records.

February 4, Year 2

Local religious groups weigh in on the issue. They defend Methodist's position that public disclosure is not required and that there is no specified, required level of charity care for Texas non-profit hospitals. The supporters are the Baptist General Convention (a statement), St. Luke's Episcopal Hospital (a letter to the editor from this Texas Medical Center neighbor), Memorial Healthcare System (a joint amicus brief), and Catholic Health Facilities (an input letter).

April 16, Year 2

After a two-month breather, Attorney General Mattox releases the AG's opinion on the Hospital's claim to be an exempt denominational organization. Now it's the AG's turn to punt. The opinion: Methodist's exemption is a "fact" question, one the courts should decide. And, the AG has no authority to require Methodist to release its records to the media. A huge sigh of relief! It seems the legal authorities in Houston and in Austin have signaled their intent to leave the Methodist issue alone.

231

March 12, Year 3

Eleven months after the AG issued his "Methodist" opinion, General Mattox proposes and finds sponsors for legislation to gain control over charitable trusts in Texas. Non-profit hospitals are charitable trusts in Texas. The legislation is subsequently rejected by Texas's Democratic legislature—a rebuff to Jim Mattox.

May 27, Year 4

Two-and-a-half years since the local TV reporter made his allegations on the 6 o'clock news, Attorney General Mattox orders the resumption of his "investigation" of The Methodist Hospital. In a letter from the AG's office, Methodist's compliance with the non-profit corporation act is challenged; charitable trust code issues are raised; and the hospital board's compliance with common-law fiduciary duties is questioned. An incredible number of documents is demanded. It is of some comfort that the letter seems to generalize the issue to a larger group of hospitals: "In view of the current healthcare crisis...this office has determined to conduct a survey of the public benefit services offered by non-profit hospitals." After checking with many hospitals around the state, we reach the conclusion that it will be a survey of one hospital—ours. The letter was released to the press at the same time as it reached us.

June 17, Year 4

Methodist delivers all requested documents to the office of the Attorney General.

July 7, Year 4

An important meeting. AG representatives meet with Methodist executives. They state that there are no allegations of illegality against Methodist. They agree to communicate this clearly to the media and the public!

July 29, Year 4

As an officer of the Texas Hospital Association (THA), I have urged an industry-wide solution to the problems of Texas charity care requirements: We have no definition of what charity care is and no agreed upon amount necessary to sustain hospital property tax exemptions. At THA's urging, Attorney General Mattox announces the creation of a "Special Task Force to Study Not-For-Profit Hospitals and Unsponsored Charity Care." The task force is established to define charity care and charitable service and determine the amount necessary to warrant tax-exemption for the state's hospitals. (This is, of course, a direct admission that such definition does not exist in current Texas law.) The composition of the task force is healthcare professionals (including a Methodist executive), community leaders, and elected officials. AG Mattox appoints himself chairman.

September 14, Year 4

The Assistant AG on our case resigns. He has been the AG's bulldog on the issue. Rumor has it that the resignation is due to his dissatisfaction with the handling of the "Methodist charity care issue."

September 23, Year 4

Another Assistant Attorney General, the new bulldog, contacts Methodist demanding the production of additional documents.

September 27, Year 4

She and her assistant visit Methodist, meet with management, and review documents. As with most visits, the press reports it.

February 24, Year 4

Five months later, Attorney General Mattox again proposes and gains sponsors for legislation to gain AG control over charitable trusts. Again, the effort fails.

March 10, Year 5

The Attorney General of Texas issues his task force's final report on unsponsored charity care in not-for-profit hospitals. It is a clear-cut victory for Methodist and the industry. It affirms our position in almost every aspect. It defines charitable services as unsponsored charity care *and* medical education, medical research, and community service expenditures (as Methodist had insisted). It recommends that no specific level of charity care be required of the state's hospitals, but that they voluntarily provide copies of their mission statements to the office of the AG. It recommends that the state Department of Health define "charitable services" and adopt a charity care reporting method. AG Mattox personally endorses the report.

May 30, Year 5

Methodist receives a letter from the Assistant AG seeking a "cooperative, not adversarial, relationship" with not-for-profit hospitals. She "applauds (Methodist's) willingness to devote time and energy to Task Force efforts." She requests a copy of Methodist's mission statement. Though the AG's office had been provided the statement in several forms in the boxes and boxes of documents we had produced at their request, we send another one.

August 4, Year 5

Methodist representatives meet with three Assistants in the AG's office in an attempt to resolve any remaining "concerns raised by the AG's review of Methodist's charity care."

August 25, Year 5

Using the recently promulgated Task Force definitions, Methodist provides the office of the Attorney General an accounting of its "unsponsored charitable" services: for 1988, $27 million in Medicare and Medicaid losses; $12 million in medical education expenses; $4.3 million in research expenses; $3.5 million in uncompensated charity care costs; and nearly $1 million in community service expenditures. A total of $48 million—far more than the pathetically small amounts claimed in news stories and by the office of the Attorney General.

October 3, Year 5

Methodist writes to the Assistant AG seeking agreement that "all open issues are resolved" and that there are "no concerns remaining regarding charitable services" provided by Methodist. The letter goes unanswered. We assume that the issue is now closed. A bad chapter in our history has been honorably concluded. It was a bad assumption. Much worse was to come.

December 21, Year 5

Attorney General Mattox files as a Democratic candidate for the office of Governor of Texas.

March 13, Year 6

Mattox is defeated in the Democratic primary in his bid to become governor. Like many conservatives, I crossed party lines to vote in the Democratic primary specifically to vote against him. He becomes lame-duck Attorney General. An angry, lame-duck Attorney General.

May 11, Year 6

Eight months after the last contact with anyone in the AG's office, the Assistant AG requests a meeting between Jim Mattox and Methodist's board leadership. The subject to be discussed? Methodist's provision of charity care.

June 22, Year 6

Our great Methodist Bishop, Ben Oliphant, Board Chairman John Bookout, and I are ushered into the imposing conference room of the Attorney General of Texas. Ranged around one end of the huge mahogany table is the entire AG staff. When we are seated, Mattox himself enters the room and stands in front of his staff and between the U.S. and Texas flags. This is not going to be a discussion meeting; this is a display of power designed to intimidate us. Mattox demands that Methodist immediately begin providing ten percent of its gross revenues in charity care—and medical education and research costs don't count. He says he has chosen us for leadership; if he can get us—the largest private non-profit hospital in the state—to do this level of charity care, the other hospitals in Texas will have to follow. He says that if we don't comply, he will bring suit. When I remind him that his own task force has a different definition of charity care and that it concluded, "It would be impossible to establish an across-the-board minimum of charitable care," he ignores me.

I looked straight at him. "General Mattox, I am one of the most law-abiding people you will ever meet. Can you show me where in the law it says a hospital must provide ten percent of gross revenues in charity care? If you can, we will begin immediately." He looked a little sheepish and said, "It is inherent in the law." The meeting was over.

July, Year 6

The performance in the AG's office has me convinced that we are the subject of a vendetta. To deal with the issue, I expand our strategic decision-making body—the Policy Council—to include the medical schools senior executives, our board's two vice chairmen, and our bishop. It now has all our leadership bases covered. We meet repeatedly to develop our response to the AG's threats. We have one set of attorneys play devil's advocate, another set play what we call angel's advocate. We invite ethicists to explore the issue with us. We prepare our position paper.

July 30, Year 6

We present our answer—our position paper—to the Attorney General. In summary, it says that Methodist was founded as a teaching and research hospital—not a charity hospital. We provide a valuable community benefit. In the prior year, we provided over $100 million in "free, uncompensated" care. The question of indigent care is a societal problem, not the responsibility of a single institution. A national healthcare policy is needed to address the issue. Following our answer to the AG, I present our paper to the editorial boards of both Houston newspapers and I give interviews to all three major television stations.

November 6, Year 6

Dan Morales is elected Attorney General of Texas.

November 26, Year 6

Just days before leaving office, in a last vengeful act, AG Mattox sues Methodist and its directors personally. The suit alleges inadequate charity care, lack of a planning process to identify and serve community needs, and violation of state revenue laws by failing to provide "requisite" charity care.

December 21, Year 6

Methodist publicly responds to the suit and denies all allegations.

December 28, Year 6

The Internal Revenue Service announces that they will begin an extensive audit of The Methodist Hospital. The audit will include an evaluation of the hospital's tax-exempt status. The all-out assault on Methodist by various branches of government has begun. Merry Christmas.

March 4, Year 7

New Attorney General Morales, pressured by Mattox's holdover staff, announces he will continue the suit.

March 21, Year 7

AG Morales initiates discovery in the lawsuit.

April 22, Year 7

Methodist responds. More than 400,000 documents are provided.

February 20, Year 8

Nearly a year later, Methodist and the AG agree to attempt mediation to settle the suit.

August, Year 8

Mediation has failed. Methodist and the AG agree to work directly, rather than through mediators, toward resolution. But, incredibly, in a face-to-face meeting, the AG staff set conditions for settlement: Methodist must establish a permanent charity care fund of at least $300 million, provide at least $30 million of charity care annually—not counting teaching and research costs—and must immediately fund a charity care project of at least $20 million. We say an emphatic "no." After all this time and effort, neither side has budged.

September 29, Year 8

AG Morales notifies Methodist that the litigation will continue.

October 30, Year 8

Methodist files a motion for summary judgment to dismiss the case.

November 23, Year 8

The AG takes my videotaped, sworn deposition and demands that I turn over to them the last ten years of my *personal* federal income tax returns. Methodist's attorneys say I don't have to do that, but it would be helpful if I did. I hand them to the AG staff. Four and a half grueling hours later, we finish.

February 19, Year 9

A state judge dismisses the AG's suit against Methodist on summary judgment. The opinion states, "The Attorney General...does not have the power to tell charitable organizations how to allocate their resources. This case is a political question...for the legislative branch of government." He found that the directors had not breached their fiduciary duty. A complete victory for Methodist! The same day, the Internal Revenue Service announced the completion of its audit of Methodist. Four full-time government auditors spent twenty-six months at the hospital to find that Methodist's tax status was correct, that there were no exemption issues, and no wrongdoing. But, punishment for our audacity in standing up to the Attorney General was still rolling in.

March 16, Year 9

Texas Department of Health (TDH) conducts an unannounced survey of Methodist Hospital in response to a "complaint from a former patient's family."

March 23, Year 9

TDH threatens to pull the hospital's Medicare contract. Citing deficiencies in "record keeping"—not patient care—TDH gives Methodist 90 days to correct the "problem."

March 30, Year 9

The Texas Senate's Health and Human Services Committee holds hearings, featuring Methodist as poster child, on the charity care issue. A Methodist executive testifies. The AG unveils its specially produced video attacking Methodist and me. After losing the lawsuit, the AG had spent thousands of dollars of taxpayer's money to try to win the public relations battle against Methodist.

March 31, Year 9

At the "request" of Congressman John Dingell, I appear before his feared Congressional Sub-committee on Investigations in Washington, D.C. Methodist is, again, the poster child—this time for the healthcare industry's "financial practices." Another witness just happened to be the Texas Assistant AG who brought along a copy of the AG attack video so that C-Span, CNN, and all the major networks could enjoy it, too.

May 3, Year 9

TDH begins a comprehensive Medicare compliance review at Methodist. Five surveyors spent three full days to determine that no complaints were validated, no compliance issues were identified, and the hospital's full Medicare deemed status was retained.

June 2, Year 9

Governor Ann Richards, who after defeating Jim Mattox in the Democratic primary went on the win the governor's race in the general election, signs into law a "community benefit" bill. Working with the Texas Hospital Association and the Texas Medical Center in Houston, we had brought the issues to the appropriate venue—the legislature— and finally had a solution to the long-fought issue. Community benefit was defined as the unreimbursed cost of charity care, medical education, and research. Reasonable required amounts for hospitals to keep their tax-exempt status were delineated. This was a victory for Texas hospitals. No longer would a vague, ill-defined standard and amount of charity care be a cloud over not-for-profit hospitals; no longer would it be a sword in unscrupulous hands to intimidate such institutions. But, for Methodist, it wasn't over quite yet.

August 13, Year 9

The film crew of the muckraking *Prime Time Live* with Sam Donaldson arrives at Methodist. They film footage of the hospital's "opulent" lobby and patient center. Sam Donaldson interviews me. This was a very narrow judgment call for me. Our public relations staff and I knew that this was another negative story about Methodist. For a national audience, to boot. With or without our participation, it was going to be bad. We decided to go ahead with the interview, but with a stipulation. Methodist wanted to videotape the interview right along with the *Prime Time Live* crew. That was one of the best public relations calls we ever made. I was extremely well prepared for the interview, and after living through this media and government assault for nine years, I was loaded for bear. At the end of the hour interview, Sam and I parted. He walked over to his producer and said, "He was prepared." We caught that on film after the interview was finished, just like the ambushing television pros do. We quickly put together a letter explaining the tape and sent the uncut interview video to all board members, other important stakeholder leaders, and to my CEO colleagues throughout the healthcare industry. When the much-edited *Prime Time* piece aired on September 30, it wasn't an issue for anyone who counted. They had seen the "whole" story. Of course, it was a brutal, heavily edited, one-sided assault on Methodist.

October 11-13, Year 9

The long, sad, and difficult saga comes to a bizarre close. Marvin Zindler, Houston's television consumer advocate—the newsman at the center of "The Best Little Whorehouse in Texas"—sees the Donaldson piece and becomes incensed. Even though he and Donaldson work for the same network, Marvin Zindler attacks Donaldson for his unfair "hatchet job" and vigorously defends Methodist. God bless Marvin Zindler!

Government doesn't fight fair.

After the nine-year fight with a powerful arm of state government was over, what were the lessons learned? There were many. They fall into these categories: policy, operational, public relations, and leadership. There were also personal lessons, for me.

From a policy perspective, we learned that good processes are essential when you find yourself publicly attacked by government and the media. And, they work together in those attacks. The local reporters and the assistants in the AG's office were in constant contact. Hiring a public relations crisis management firm at the very beginning was important to our organization's thought processes. Our initial response to the opening salvo was the basis for all future position papers and responses. The most important process, though, was the role of our expanded Policy Council. All the important board, medical staff, medical school, and executive leaders were there, calmly working through the issues, our responses, and their consequences.

From an operational perspective, the case was very disruptive—as you can imagine. First, it is very demoralizing to see an organization you are very proud of constantly being attacked by the state and the media. Then there were all the disruptions in everyday work because of case-related meetings, document production, and policy analysis. And, it impacted the budget. It was expensive in employees' time and in lawyer and consultant fees.

Communicate! That was the public relations lesson learned. Communicate internally: We learned to quickly respond to allegations; to tell the whole story; and to promote unity, loyalty, and morale. Communicate externally: We learned to always respond publicly and to answer each and every allegation. High profile lawsuits are tried in two courts: the court of law and the court of public opinion. We absolutely dominated the issue in the court of law, but we got badly mauled in the media. Charity care is a ready-made political sound bite; it is an issue that is made for demagogy and demonizing. While we were right legally and ethically, we were in a fight with politicians who didn't play fair. Interestingly, bad press is not always bad for business. Throughout the entire struggle, the public perception of Methodist remained exceedingly strong.

We learned that large, prestigious, leadership institutions are targets. The dragon slayers don't go after small dragons, they want the big guys. If they can kill the largest dragon in the forest, they can easily mop up the little ones. We were large, very financially successful, and prestigious—plus from the Attorney General's point of view, we had the added advantage of being in Houston, not his hometown of Dallas. Methodist was the big dragon. The second leadership lesson was: it is lonely on the point. It is no fun being the target of controversial and emotional issues. While many colleagues in the industry expressed sympathy and support for our position, not many ran to join our side in battle. I felt that some were glad it was us on the point, not them. I felt that some took quiet pleasure that the mighty Methodist was being roughed up in a dirty political fight.

The personal lessons I learned were painful, but they helped me grow as a leader. I, the CEO, was scrutinized and attacked because, if the AG could find something criminal or unethical about me, he could pressure me to make my organization do his bidding. I learned that in a shootout like this one, I needed to be squeaky clean. My handling of personal taxes, business expenses, and business relationships were all put under the microscope. And, the institution needed to be squeaky clean, as well. Thank heavens there were no personal or institutional improprieties. Had there been, they would have been found.

I learned that it is not easy to do the right thing. It's not cheap. In fact, as I found out, it can be very expensive. And, doing the right thing isn't necessarily appreciated. When the attacks first began, one of my directors told me that I should settle at all costs as soon as possible; the institution had 50 years of sterling reputation and I was ruining it. He wasn't a run-of-the-mill board member either. And finally, I learned that it isn't easy to fight government. And, government doesn't fight fair. Government has unlimited time and resources. They have tremendous power and all of the stature and influence of office. When they and their collaborators in the press bring it all to bear on you and your organization, it is awesome and frightening.

If I had it all to do over again, would I do it differently? Over drinks in a hotel in Washington, D.C., following the grilling I had gone through at the hands of John Dingell's committee, that was the gist of the question posed by my attorney. Craig Smyser had been through most of the long, bloody fight with us and we were both pretty tired—of the long day and the long fight. I said yes. I would fight it all over again. Craig look surprised and a little like he thought I wasn't capable of learning from bad experience. We didn't stay up to discuss it further. Now years later, after more reflection, the answer is still yes.

In the middle of the fight, another attorney acquaintance of mine—a criminal lawyer—said to me, "Remember, Larry, you can beat the rap, but you can't beat the ride." Or as another friend summed it up: Methodist was right on the issue—dead right. He meant that we won the legal case, but got killed in the press. Well, I'd lead down that path again, because we were right and it was important for us to prove it! Not just for Methodist, but also for all not-for-profit hospitals in the state. Methodist handily beat the rap; the ride was dirty, bruising, and miserable, but we survived it. Methodist got a lot of criticism in the press, but in the end a clarifying law resulted.

Finally, when public officials try to pressure institutions to do their political will, in the absence of statutory authority— or when they tell you it is "inherent" in the law—someone should stop them.

Education

You can teach an old dog new tricks.
But, you really shouldn't.

There is dignity in an old dog. You see it in the way he walks, the way he wags his tail when he greets you at the door; it's not the way it was when he was young and frisky, it's slower, more understanding, and more genuine. Teach a young dog a trick and he is all hustle and full of himself. Try to teach an old dog a new trick, you see a resigned willingness; you know he will try to learn it, but there is that pathetic look in his eyes. They woefully ask, "Hasn't my time for new tricks passed?"

There comes a time when executives are like old dogs, when their time for new things has passed. It doesn't necessarily come with age, though it certainly can arrive that way. I have seen executives burned out, worn down, used up, consumed and spent. Many were older, veteran executives, but some were relatively young. It eventually happens to most of us. Leadership is an all-consuming occupation that can sap your energy, take your vitality, and even ruin your health. It requires continuous learning, adaptation, and change. There comes a time when it is over. You do not have the ability to continue effectively; your time for learning new tricks is passed.

Moving on is your last act of true leadership. Don't condemn yourself. You knew when you became an executive that it was going to be heavy lifting; you knew, also, that someday it would be over. Be true to yourself and good to your followers by passing the torch to the next generation of leaders. And, as you go, do it with at least as much dignity as an old dog.

We require not continuing education,
but continuous education.

When I graduated from college, I bought an unabridged dictionary and a one-volume encyclopedia. I thought they were the only general references I would ever need. Today, I sit in front of a blinking screen above a keyboard and have access to the accumulated knowledge of mankind.

In only 200 years, Americans have passed through the agricultural, industrial, and service ages and now are rushing from the information age to the much-touted electronic one. It has been reported that Americans today make more decisions and choices in a month than their grandparents did in a lifetime.

In the United States, we live our lives at warp speed, pagers attached to our belts and cell phones glued to our ears, jetting from continent to continent, e-mailing and faxing orders and queries on our laptops. The explosion of knowledge in all professions is so great that one's graduate education is obsolete as soon as the degree is granted. And, the American healthcare industry has reached unbelievable degrees of complexity.

As an executive, managing and leading complex organizations like hospitals in the information age is much more challenging than managing and leading in any other age. The idea that you can maintain your knowledge base and your competency through annual or semi-annual continuing education doses is, on its face, ridiculous. You live in a world requiring you to learn daily just to stay even. To remain

251

relevant and competent, you must alter your view of education from something formally imparted to a continuous learning process. Treat every encounter, every meeting, and every moment as an educational experience. Don't ever let a moment pass without learning. If you aren't learning something new about your profession, learn something new about leadership. Learn something new about followers. Learn something new about you.

If you aren't in a self-directed continuous education program, you are in the process of becoming as obsolete as a man in the freight-hauling business with a horse and wagon competing against someone with a train.

Ethics

Know where the line is drawn within you.
Don't ever cross it.

In the final analysis, what you are inside is all you have. Is integrity there? Is honesty? Do you know where your line between right and wrong is drawn? Would you cross it? For money? For opportunity? For fame? Would you do something you knew to be wrong, but of great benefit to you, if you were guaranteed never to be found out? These are questions for the man in the mirror. How does he look when they are posed? How does he answer when it is just the two of you, face to face?

I believe that most executives are well grounded in ethics, respect the law, and know right from wrong. They know where the line is drawn within themselves. Most of those who get in ethical or legal trouble have made a conscious decision to cross that interior line. When that happens, even if they are never caught, they have violated themselves in the most fundamental way.

In your career as an executive, you will encounter many legal and ethical dilemmas. They will not all be black and white situations; there will be an array of shades of gray. If you are to walk successfully through the minefield, you must clearly know where the line between right and wrong is drawn in you. Do not ever cross it. In your career, and in your life, others may violate you. They may abuse you, cheat you, injure you, slander you, or even kill you. But all of that is nothing compared to what you do to yourself when you consciously walk across that line from right to wrong.

You must clearly know when to walk away. You must walk away from money. You must walk away from promotion. You must walk away from opportunity. You must walk away from fame. If the price is crossing the line in you, you must walk away. If you don't, you will never again be able to meet the gaze of the man in the mirror.

Once you know a thing, you can't unknow it.

As an executive, you learn about many things you don't want to: Hypothetically, an anonymous letter says your highest admitting physician is on cocaine; a job applicant accuses your personnel director of making sexual advances; a fellow executive, your best friend in the organization, brags about padding his expense account; an assistant comes to your office to tell you in confidence that her boss, a prominent physician researcher, is intentionally falsifying results on his National Institutes of Health research protocol. As much as you would prefer not to have to deal with these things (many of which may not be in your areas of direct responsibility), once you know them, you own them.

Throughout my executive career, I learned things about people and my organization that I would rather not have learned. These things came in gossip, in confidential conversations, and in anonymous letters. When they were about the personal lives of colleagues and did not have a bearing on the organization, I did nothing about them. But, when they had implications for Methodist, I tried to immediately validate the truth of the matter and, if appropriate, take corrective action. Many times, I knew that doing so would have serious negative public relations, regulatory, or legal consequences for the organization and might reflect poorly on me as well. But, I took action anyway. I acted because I was an executive with fiduciary and stewardship responsibility and I knew that if I failed to act, I would be complicit. As much as I might have preferred not to know these things, once I knew them, I could not unknow them.

As an executive, you are a principal steward of the organization. You cannot put your head in the sand. Or, assume the unwelcome information is simply untrue. You cannot pretend that you do not know. You cannot hope that someone else will deal with it. You must act. First, fairly and carefully investigate the truth of the situation. Many rumors are untrue, or at least are not totally true. Lives, jobs, careers, and reputations are at stake. A blunderbuss approach to getting at the truth does not serve you or the organization well. Each situation will probably require its own unique approach to fact finding. If you confirm the truth of the matter, you must act to change the behavior and to protect the organization. That involves notifying the appropriate organizational authorities, perhaps the police, perhaps regulators. If a crime has been committed, it cannot be punished by an organizational slap on the wrist; it must be reported. If organizational money has been misappropriated, not only must the crime be punished, the money must be recouped. It is an executive's fiduciary duty.

These are situations that are extraordinarily difficult and painful. It is never easy to admit that your organization has such problems, much less report them to organizational authorities, the police, or regulatory bodies. But, the organization must know that its leaders take their fiduciary and stewardship responsibilities very seriously. Employees, physicians, board members, and volunteers must see and have confidence that once their executives know a thing, they won't try to unknow it, forget it, or bury it. Action must be taken. It is a matter of stewardship. It is a matter of leadership. It is matter of ethics.

People can rationalize anything.

Some of the German people who knew of Hitler's atrocities still supported him. They said he tamed inflation, made their trains run on time, and built their autobahns. Adolph Eichmann, the head Nazi exterminator of the Jews during World War Two, justified his actions as "only following orders." In America, in an attempt to save his presidency and remain in office, President Nixon went on national television and told us: "I am not a crook," as if cover-ups and obstruction of justice were not quintessentially "crooked." President Bill Clinton explained his lying under oath in the Paula Jones lawsuit as necessary to protect his marriage.

Such prominent examples have helped convince me that people have an unlimited ability to devise self-satisfying, but incorrect, reasons for self-serving behavior—the definition of rationalization. My experience with the behavior of a few executive colleagues around the country reinforced that belief. I knew of several who sent employees of their organizations to their homes to do repair or construction work. Their explanation? They were too busy working on behalf of their organizations to handle things at home. Any number of self-serving dips into the assets of their organizations for their personal use were explained away because "I have given my life to this organization." Using a not-for-profit hospital's paper, stamps, and secretarial time to prepare and send a boy scout mailing for a son's troop, is explained away as "it's for a good cause."

All of us have a very well developed sense of what is in our best self-interest. We generally know what we like and want—usually more things, more power, more sex, and more money. Executives are put in charge of an organization's assets, which if converted to their personal use, can potentially enhance their gain of all of these things. And, with the power to rationalize, that conversion to personal use can be explained and justified in dazzlingly creative ways. Unfortunately, they are all wrong. There is *no* rational basis for appropriating the organization's assets for personal use.

As an executive you are given a position of trust and stewardship. If you are tempted to ask an employee to pick up your laundry for you, ask your secretary to type a personal letter for you, make personal copies on the office copier, or take home office supplies, you call into question that trust and stewardship. If you can find within yourself good reasons for doing these things, you are rationalizing. There are *no* good reasons for abusing your position of trust and stewardship.

All of us want good things for ourselves. But, as executives, we must constantly separate our personal wants and needs from our decisions about the organization's people and assets. If you begin to confuse what is good for you with what is good for the organization, it might help to reflect that, when it comes to our self-interest, people can rationalize anything. And, "anything" covers a hideously wide range of human behavior.

An organization and its executives' finances are like fire and gunpowder. Don't mix them.

Which of the following is bad executive practice?

a. The boss brings his daughter to the office to sell Girl Scout cookies to his staff.

b. The boss instructs human resources to hire her teenager for a summer job.

c. The boss hires his wife as an assistant in the corporate offices.

d. The boss arranges for the organization to loan him several hundred thousand dollars, interest free.

e. The boss arranges for the company to purchase his home, upon his departure from the organization, at a predetermined, fixed price, regardless of the real estate market at the time.

f. The boss' wife owns and operates the hospital gift shop.

g. The boss is a silent partner in a construction firm that provides services to the hospital.

The answer? All of the above.

They range from bad leadership—placing staff members in an uncomfortable and untenable position—(a, b, and c) to inappropriate mixing of personal and corporate assets (d and e) and to serious conflicts of interest (f and g). Let's examine one of the situations in each group.

First, bad leadership—asking the human resources department to hire your teenage daughter. Questions of her qualifications and need for her services are eliminated by your request. Can other employees in the company do the same for their sons or daughters? Once she has been placed in an operating unit, you give the unit manager your speech: "I want this young woman to be treated just like any other employee. I want her to work hard and learn what it takes to earn a dollar. Don't do her any favors just because he is my daughter." Great speech. Sets just the right tone, doesn't it? Not exactly. Here's what the unit manager heard: "I am the boss. I have waived all the rules to have my child placed in your department. She is going to be here every day for an entire summer seeing everything that goes on in your area. Things had better go well. If they don't, I will certainly hear about it at home. And, I'm sure she will have an opinion about your leadership, as well."

Let's assume that everything goes splendidly. The young woman is a paragon of virtue and wins praise for her pleasing manner and hard work. What will employees throughout the organization think? They will believe that she was given special consideration and high marks because she was the boss' daughter. And, if things don't go well? Will the disciplinary procedure really be used in the same manner it would be for any other employee? If it somehow is, what happens when it goes all the way—to you, the boss, the final authority? In either circumstance, you have placed your subordinates in an untenable position and have raised questions in your employees' minds about using the organization for your family's benefit.

The second group of questions deals with mixing your personal financial affairs with the organization's assets. What happens when you, the boss, arrange a no-interest loan from your employer—say a not-for-profit hospital? It is frequently done, often in ignorance of and contravention of state laws to the contrary. How does it look to your employees that you, most likely the highest paid person in the corporation, don't go get a bank or credit union loan at commercial rates as each of them is expected to do? Since it is a no-interest loan, you are rightly viewed as depriving the organization of the proper return on that money. And, you are supposed to be the one with the highest fiduciary duty to protect its assets.

Finally, there are outright conflicts of interest that raise serious ethical red flags. If you, or a member of your immediate family, are involved in any business that sells services to your organization, you are in conflict. Even fully approved by the board and widely disclosed, the practice will continually raise questions about propriety. And, of course, employees making decisions about the business relationship between the vendor and the organization will never forget that the boss has a personal interest in this vendor.

Your personal financial business and your family, in these circumstances, are gunpowder. Your organization is fire. If you mix the two, there is a very high probability of a nasty, public flash. And, somebody is going to get burned.

Honesty is the only policy.

"Honesty is the best policy" is a very common adage. For executives, it is not appropriate. The "best" implies that there are other acceptable policies with honesty being at the top of the list. I do not believe that for an organization's leaders there are acceptable alternatives; for them, honesty must be the *only* policy.

Honest is a simple word, but it carries a nobility of meaning. Here is how *The American Heritage Dictionary* defines it: "Marked by or displaying integrity, upright; Not deceptive or fraudulent, genuine; Equitable, fair; Characterized by truth, not false; Sincere, frank; Of good repute; Respectable. Exhibiting goodness and decency, scrupulous, ethical, aboveboard."

Outstanding leadership requires a very special relationship between a leader and his followers. A boss' deception, fraud, unfairness, or lies more than undermine that relationship, they destroy it. Followers trust that their leaders will act with honesty, integrity, and fairness. When they learn that is not the case, that trust—so essential to the relationship— withers and dies. With it leadership dies.

"He was an upright leader, full of integrity. He was genuine and not deceptive; his decisions were fair and equitable. He was sincere and frank; he spoke only the truth. He had a sterling reputation; he was respectable, good, decent, scrupulous, ethical, and aboveboard." If this were said of you at the end of your career as an executive, you could count your career a smashing success. If those words were in your obituary, generations of your heirs would recount your virtues. If the words were reversed and the opposite were said, you could not claim to have been a leader and you should not look a leader in the eye.

It is the first, last, and only thing for which there is no alternative: a leader must be honest. Honest—in the fullness of that word.

There is no shame in accepting the blame
for doing the right thing.

In organizations, telling the truth, behaving ethically, obeying the law, and doing what is fair and right are not always appreciated. They are not always popular. They can, in fact, be downright disruptive. The executive who acts ethically, but thereby disrupts the organization, can face considerable condemnation.

Fire a popular, long-tenured middle manager for an ethical breach? Her friends in the organization will not thank you for it.

Report a high revenue-producing surgeon to Medicare for fraud and abuse? His fellow physicians may not be too pleased with you.

Stop the company-subsidized day care program, because it is an unfair benefit serving only one class of employees—those with children? You may be accused of sexism or lack of compassion for working mothers.

Speak honestly to the board about inappropriate board member conflicts of interest? You may stir up enough animosity that eventually they fire you—for something else, of course.

Doing the right thing can be difficult and have unpleasant consequences. By acting ethically, you might significantly reduce revenues, bring unwanted media attention, or involve your organization with law-enforcement agencies. That is unfortunate for the organization, but it can also be difficult for you and your career, as well. You might lose your friends and supporters, you might lose your bonus, you might lose your raise, and you might lose your job. All of that, just for doing what's right? Unfortunately, sometimes yes.

I do not advocate that you be a Jeremiah, a loudly proclaiming prophet of organizational doom. Or that you present yourself as a tactless, blunt instrument for right. I do not advocate that you abandon the search for compromise solutions to thorny problems. And, legal and ethical questions can be thorny problems. But, with tact, grace, and persistence work through them. In the end, though, there can be no compromise in doing what is legally and ethically right. When it is unpopular, when it is disruptive, and when they are pointing the finger squarely at you, know that, when you have done right, blame does not bring shame.

Life

There are other kinds of worth than net.

When I was a pre-teenager, my father assigned me household chores, and if I properly performed them, he gave me a weekly allowance of $2.50. It wasn't all that much, but in addition, my father insisted I give 25 cents a week to the Southern Baptist Church. When I complained, he said that if I gave my tithe to the church, the Lord would bless me financially. I asked him how I could be sure of that. He said, "Because, I am the agent of the Lord."

When my daughter, Julie, was about the same age, one of my relatives came to visit us in Houston. After the visit, Julie said to me, "Honestly, Dad, your relatives. All they want is our money." I said to my brash daughter, "Tell me Julie, how did they get to be my relatives and how did it get to be our money?"

When I told my sister, JoEllen, that money couldn't buy happiness, she said, "That's what rich people say. Give me some money. It might not buy me happiness, but it'll make a down payment on it for me."

When I was first stationed in Europe as a 22-year old lieutenant, *Europe on Five Dollars a Day* was a best-selling guidebook. As we traveled during my leaves, we followed it scrupulously. We proved it could be done—a necessity on a lieutenant's pay. Now when we get to Europe, I accuse my wife, Diane, of writing a sequel, *Europe on a Thousand*

Dollars a Day. She doesn't confirm or deny the project, but does note that that wouldn't include drinks.

Money! After water, food, shelter and sex, it is the next primal need. People work for it, cheat for it, gamble for it, and steal it. It is the ultimate cliché maker: The love of money is the root of all evil, money makes the world go round. People dream and scheme about it. While they fear the odds of being killed in an airplane crash, they happily spend good money for tickets in lotteries with much worse odds. We all have our own very special relationship with money. We must come to terms with money, because we cannot live without it.

In the United States, money is a surrogate for success and, by extension, individual worth. If a person has money in America, he or she is viewed as "somebody." Regardless of personal qualities—whether honest, ethical, trustworthy, or not—the rich person is seen as successful. But, far too often, that is not an accurate view.

As an executive, you are going to make more money than the average person. It is important that you come to terms with your money. Here are some attitudes that you might consider:

- Never work for money, work for your profession. The money will take care of itself.

- Never live up to your income. Keep your standard of living well below your compensation. You will save more for the future that way and you will not become accustomed to a lifestyle that you won't be able to afford later in life.

- Never define yourself in terms of your wealth. Judge your personal success on your integrity, your relationship with family and friends, and your fidelity to those you lead.

Money is important. A substantial net worth means a comfortable life, the opportunity to help others through charitable giving, and the ability to take care of your family now and after you are gone. But, there are other kinds of worth than net worth. What are you worth to your wife or husband? What are you worth to your children? What are you worth to your church? What are you worth to your community? What are you worth to the organization you lead? When next you run the numbers on your net worth statement, take a little time to run the values of those other kinds of worth. If they dwarf your net worth, count yourself "somebody" in America.

Life is a series of offsetting influences.

An executive's work is all about choices. You lead the decision-making processes for your organization. And, it is fun and rewarding to make choices: Who will be promoted, what new program will be funded, what strategy will be pursued? Good leaders give considerable thought to those choices, before they make them. *Great* leaders give an equal amount of thought to the consequences of those choices. Every choice, in an organization and in life, has consequences, both foreseeable and unforeseen.

When you decide to promote an employee, ask yourself what other employees might leave the organization, because they believed they should have been the one promoted. When you choose to fund a new program, ask yourself where else might these funds be used productively. When you pursue a strategic course, ask yourself what other strategic option is this one crowding out. When you choose to work 70-hour weeks, ask yourself what is this doing to your marriage, your kids.

Every choice you make will cause a reaction somewhere. Every choice you make will eliminate other possible choices. And, while you will do well to ponder the reactions and the eliminated options along with the decisions themselves, you must know that you cannot anticipate all of the consequences. It is the unanticipated consequences that cause most of the heartaches. It is also those unforeseen consequences that make leadership and life interesting and exciting.

Life is not a dress rehearsal.

There are many sayings that express this thought. Calvin, of Calvin and Hobbes, says "Life is short; play naked." My daughter, Jennifer, who lives a worry-free life, once told me: "Life is too short to worry about the important things." One Christmas, she gave me a book that contained this adage: "Days are long; life is short." But the one I like best is what Diane told me as we discussed our future together, "Life is not a dress rehearsal, Larry."

I first learned those basic truths while in college, listening to my parents' talk of retirement, when neither of them would work and they would travel and live the good life. Mom never quit working and she died at age 54 of a heart attack. There was no retirement together, no travel, no good life. And, later, I had the truth of these sayings brought home to me in a dramatic and frightening way.

August, 1991. It is a hot, bright, Saturday morning in my neighborhood in Houston. I check my gold Rolex watch; it is 8:30 a.m. "Come on, JoEllen, time's a-wasting." My sister is staying at my house and she and I have errands to run prior to tomorrow's departure for a family beach vacation. We load the dirty laundry in the car and start out. Our first stop is the drive-through window at the bank where I got cash for the trip. Next stop, the dry cleaners. Finally, we stop at Randall's, the big, new supermarket where we pick up food supplies to take on vacation. As I pull back into my driveway at home, I wave to my neighbors' little girls playing in the front yard next door.

I grab the clean laundry from the backseat and go into the house, leaving my sister to unload the groceries.

"Larry, there is a guy here who wants to talk to you," JoEllen yelled.

I went to the side door of my house, where a man stood in my driveway. "Yes, Sir," I said, "What can I do for you?" He looked odd, somehow.

"I'm looking for yard work," he said.

"I'm sorry," I said, "I have a fellow whose been doing my yard for me for years. Have a good day." I turned and went upstairs to finish putting away the laundry.

"Larry, this guy wants to talk to you again," JoEllen called.

I walked down the stairs, through the kitchen, to the side door. The man is still standing where I left him minutes ago. I'm beginning to get a strange feeling. "Do you discriminate in this neighborhood?" he asked.

"Oh, no, this is a great neighborhood. You can ask about work at any of these homes." As I said the last few words, he reached behind his back, pulled an automatic pistol from his waistband, and clasping it in both hands a foot away from my face, pointed it right between my eyes.

As a former combat officer, my first and only thought was "he's going to kill me." I jumped to my left, slammed the door in his face, spun into the kitchen, hurled a butcher-block table behind me and started to run. He was right behind me. I sensed he was going to shoot then, so I dove for the floor. That's where he caught up with me. As I lay there, he once again put the gun in my face and said, "Give me your watch." Relief flooded through me! While the watch cost several thousand dollars, it was just a watch he wanted. He didn't want to kill me. I immediately, unclasped it and handed it to him.

But, he didn't move the gun from my face.

I heard my sister screaming out in the driveway from where she had seen the whole thing. I heard the children playing next door. I realized that my life was about to end. "Please, don't kill me," I said. An eternity later—in fact, probably only a few seconds later—he slowly moved the gun from my face, turned and ran through the kitchen and out of the house.

The Houston Rolex robberies, we later learned, were well-coordinated affairs. At an upscale store like Randall's, an accomplice would spot a man wearing a gold Rolex watch and follow him to his car. Using a cell phone, he would call the gunman, who was circling in a car, describe the departing car and identify which street it was taking. The gunman followed and did the rest. In Houston, about half of those robbed of their Rolexes were also killed. I think I was spared because my sister had seen everything and was screaming bloody murder outside.

I never got the watch back. They never caught the gunman. I never bought another watch that someone would kill me for. Every day after that day was a gift.

When you are born, the curtain rises on a unique play. You are in the spotlight at center stage—the unrehearsed Star! The play will run only once and, strangely, neither the on-lookers nor the Star know how or when it will end. My play could have ended as a car struck me at my fifth birthday party, with pneumonia in a Colorado hospital, on my motorbike under the wheels of a station wagon, in the rice paddies of Vietnam, in my own emergency room with chest pains, or years later in a coronary care unit in Turkey. Or, it could have ended on a bright August Saturday morning lying on the floor of my home with the sound of children playing outside, at the point of a gun. But, none called down the final curtain. They all were only the dramatic closings of the acts.

So, how do you play this one-time show? Do not make it a comedy. Do not make it a tragedy. Make it an exciting drama. Play the love scenes with sensitivity and passion. When good confronts evil, wear the white hat—lead the forces of good to triumph. And, when the death scene comes, do not meet the grim reaper cowering and whimpering, but square your shoulders and boldly meet his gaze. We all must meet him: Let your last scene be brave. Play the lead with confidence and honesty, with style and grace. Be all the Star you can be! And, when that final curtain descends, they will say, "Bravo. Well done!" They will say it was a smash hit.

Today is not forever.

This is the greatest truth I have learned. It is in some ways the most reassuring. In some ways the most threatening. Not understanding it is a prescription for a difficult career and, perhaps, an unhappy and confused life.

When I was in high school in rural southeastern Kansas, I had a wonderful English teacher. One of the stories she led us to was the tale of caravan travelers finding the base of a colossal statue in the desert. It was huge. Their minds boggled at the thought of the statue that must have stood on that platform. But of that statue, there was no trace. On one side of the base was this inscription in an ancient language: "This too shall pass." What a powerful ruler must have erected such a monument. What a wise ruler must have known even his greatest works would fade and disappear. I carefully hand lettered "This too shall pass," framed it, and hung it on my wall. It stayed on walls of mine through high school, college, and army years. It was comforting when tests didn't produce As, Bs, or Cs, when love relationships soured, when money was scarce, when the AK-47 bullets whizzed too close and the exploding mortar rounds walked karump, karump, karump in a straight line toward me. When I was down, when I was depressed, when I was sad, when the professional mountain to climb couldn't appear any steeper or more difficult, when the future couldn't appear any more veiled and uncertain, knowing that those times would pass was a comfort.

On the bright spring days of my youth, when all was right in my world, when the meadow was golden, the stream sparkling silver, the bees nuzzling the yellow wild flowers, and when a girl I loved laughed beside me as we lay on our picnic blanket, a small voice reminded: "This too shall pass." Not a threat; a promise.

In the CEO chair, surrounded by admiring and respecting executives and employees, making important decisions about important matters, amid the lavish accouterments of the corner office, the voice whispered.

I have modernized that hand-lettered promise—so ancient, so mystical, so true, "This too shall pass"—to "Today is not forever." Believing that today's state will go on in perpetuity is common. It is a mistake made by corporate planners who project that the next five year's sales growth will be an average of the last two year's record-shattering pace. It is a mistake made by professional athletes who believe that their phenomenal physical condition and their stratospheric incomes will last forever. "Today is not forever" is the time-proven promise of change.

If things are good today, they will change. If things are bad today, they will change. Will the good times of today change for the worse? Will the bad times of today change for the better? Of course, we, as human beings and as executives, do not know. Good times may get worse. Good times may get even better. Bad times may get better. Bad times may get even worse. What will happen, will happen. We can not predict the future. But, we can, with assurance, assert that things will change.

The lesson in this is that each of us must learn to live with, manage with, and overcome our fear of the promise and certainty of change. Failure to understand that *all* things change sets us up for shocks and bumps and surprises in our lives and mistakes and bad leadership in our professions. It leads us to unrealistic expectations. It puts irreconcilable pressures on relationships. It leads to bad strategy, worse tactics, and flawed leaderships in the executive suite. Change is not easy to accept in concept; it is even worse to live with in fact. We all are resistant to change—particularly if things are going well, if things are working, if we feel comfortable and secure. Change is threatening. We do not know what will happen when change comes; and, uncertainty is frightening. Indeed, the pain of uncertainty is worse than certain pain. But, somehow, if we are to live successful lives and have productive careers, we must find détente with change. It would be pretty to think that all of us could make change our friend, as some of the trendy management books advise; but, for most of us in the executive suite, that probably is not possible. It may be enough that we get control of the physical and psychic effects of change on us. As in combat, the infantryman in the mud never loses his fear; he overcomes it to do what is required of him. At the very least, we can intellectually and viscerally accept the truth of the promise of change.

Today is not forever. This too shall pass.

Life begins at 40—and lasts for 24 hours.

We had canoed all day on the pristine Current River in central Missouri and now we were sitting around the campfire on a sand bar. We were six army officers, all combat veterans, off on a stag weekend. We had finished a dinner of steak and lobster tails and were now relaxing and finishing the red wine. Pete looked pensive as he put ice cubes into his wine glass. He was thirty-two, the second oldest of the group. Other than the colonel, we were all in our twenties. "What are you thinking about?" I asked. He smiled ruefully and said, "This red wine on ice. The last time I drank red wine on ice was on my thirtieth birthday in Vietnam. That was one hell of a party— lasted all night long. I found out life begins at 30—and lasts 24 hours." We roared. We had all had nights like that, too. We were twenty-somethings who understood the humor of a life shattering hangover, but we didn't get the wisdom of it.

A few years later, I thought life began at 40 as I assumed the chief executive role. What a wonderful feeling it was. But I was brought up short as I began a round of surgeries to correct the results of youthful activities—pole-vaulting and parachuting. I had arthroscopic surgery on each knee, both a cervical and a lumbar laminectomy, and a shoulder operation. At 44, I had my first heart attack and began my lifelong argument with heart disease, which has led to five catheterizations, four angioplasties, three stents, and one subsequent heart attack. As soon as I had it made and was enjoying life to the fullest, life pulled aside the veil and showed me the end.

Whether in your 30s, 40s, 50s, 60s, 70s, or 80s, at some point you will confront your 24 hours. I can honestly say, for me each decade has been better than the one before. The joys of beginning a career were exceeded by the satisfaction of ending one well. The joys of parenthood were eclipsed by the rapture of grandparenthood. The striving of a first marriage was replaced by the bliss of a second. I count my life blessed that it has been this way. I think part of it was that I was forced to confront the twenty-four hours rule early in my life. It made every day that much sweeter. If you haven't had a life-altering event that has made you see the end, you are lucky. At some point, you will. My counsel to you in the meantime: Enjoy your life and count your blessings as if your time left was in hours.

And, every so often, drink just a little red wine on ice.

The Author

In 1997, Larry L. Mathis chose to retire at the age of 54. He left at the peak of a highly successful career in health care leadership. He has served as CEO of the Methodist Hospital System in Houston, with its 7,000 employees and a 1,000+ bed, flagship hospital. His peers elected him to lead the industry's two prestigious organizations—the American Hospital Association and the American College of Healthcare Executives. He was deluged with job offers when the announcement was made, but turned down all of them.

Today, Larry revels in doing the kinds of things that don't require suits, ties and shoes with tassels. He works with selected clients as a leadership consultant with D. Peterson & Associates, his wife's Houston-based health care consulting firm. He also serves as a member of the board of Sulzer Medica, an international high technology and medical device corporation headquartered in Zurich, Switzerland.

He and Diane continue to travel extensively, even after having reached their goal of setting foot on each of the world's continents.

Acknowledgements

Special thanks to my first editor, Susan Anthony; wrapup editor Nancy Peacock Jensen; and production assistant Jeanette Marchant for their invaluable work on the manuscript.